Contents

P9-DUH-761

Preface ix
Acknowledgments xiii

1 Lessons From a Roads Scholar — 1

Five of the most important lessons you can learn to reach your potential

2 Stride Mechanics — 23

Improve your posture, leg turnover, arm swing, and breathing technique to become more efficient

3 Psychomechanics — 47

Develop mental focusing techniques to run faster and more easily

4 Mind and Body Control — 81

Manage your thoughts and emotions and learn to control your physical responses during competition

5 Competitive Mindset — 101

Create a mental blueprint to meet the challenges of each competition

6 Performance Programming — 117

Preparation and assessment strategies to implement your blueprint and achieve extraordinary results on race day

Bibliography 151
Index 153
About the Author 159

Preface

I've spent many years developing the material presented in *Programmed to Run.* I was initially motivated to learn the secrets of better running and racing performance so that I could improve my own running efficiency; later, my incentive was to help the athletes with whom I work. As a sport science student, researcher, and educator, however, I became frustrated with the lack of texts that provide an interdisciplinary sport science approach to enhancing athletic performance. To reach your personal potential, you must train your mind and body collaboratively, but most running books don't cover how to improve mechanics and develop mental coping techniques to perform better.

Programmed to Run weaves together elements of exercise physiology, sport psychology, biomechanics, and motor learning to help you understand and apply the mind/body connection. Runners at all levels, from beginning to advanced, running distances from the mile to the marathon, will learn how to improve both physical and mental running skills to achieve extraordinary results.

Chapter 1, "Lessons From a Roads Scholar," is a personal account that illustrates five important running lessons. This chapter takes you through the step-by-step development of performance principles based on my own running, racing, and coaching experiences during nearly 40 years of searching for the secrets of better running. The core revelation contained in these principles is that your running and racing potential is founded on *how you run*—literally. Without efficient, biomechanically sound running technique, you will be dogged by chronic injury, unable to sustain consistently progressive training programs, and disappointed by your performance. Because past and current running publications and books place so little emphasis on developing sound technique, those runners who excel are naturally gifted. This chapter, however, demonstrates how runners with less natural ability can develop physical and mental running skills to mimic the talent of the elites. Applying these skills leads to fewer injuries, more consistent training, faster racing, and greater satisfaction and joy from the simple act of running!

Chapter 2, "Stride Mechanics," explains the elements of efficient running. It reviews literature and research to support the recommended stride dynamics patterns. Sequential photographs of miler Jim Ryun will help you observe and analyze the technique of an elite runner. Anyone willing to take the time and effort can learn and adopt economy of movement. The chapter specifically discusses elements of efficient mechanical technique, supplemental energy sources, and breathing skills.

Understanding the elements of efficient running biomechanics and integrating these elements into your motor habits are separate but related skills. Chapter 3, "Psychomechanics," presents a number of strategies to refine your physical/mental running skills. How you think influences how you run, and *psychomechanics* refers to the art of programming your mind to direct your physical movements accurately. Because each of us learns in a slightly different way, the chapter addresses several modes of thinking. Even if you are a natural runner, effective focusing strategies are essential to keep you from losing your focus in the latter part of races or hard training sessions. Your racing will always reflect your training and preparation strategies. This chapter discusses a variety of traditional and nontraditional training methods. You'll learn how to

- assess your current running technique;
- develop and refine psychomechanical skills;
- apply psychomechanical skills to run faster and more easily; and
- train to improve speed, power, and endurance.

Chapter 4, "Mind and Body Control," helps you understand how your mind works and how you can better manage it as you prepare and perform. Elite athletes have more effective strategies for dealing with their inner critics, and therefore they control their attention and manage their emotions better. You can learn mental skills to give yourself better control in performance situations.

Chapter 5, "Competitive Mindset," analyzes the conflicting forces that act on your mind before and during events, and it explains how to manage them effectively to optimize your performances. A performance blueprint is presented to help you understand how you can better manage your mind during performing situations.

It's not enough to have refined your biomechanics and psychomechanics if you show up for the race at the wrong time, if you have the wrong shoes or gear, or if you don't know about the long uphill finish. The secret of consistent performance—and the key to unlocking your performance potential—is preparing to meet the functional (course-specific), physical, mental, social, logistical, technical, and environmental demands for each race. In chapter 6, "Performance Programming," you'll learn to put it all together. This "how-to" presentation takes you from the decision to enter the big race through the preparation process, performance planning, program execution, and post-event assessments. After digesting the information in this chapter, you will be ready to be your own head coach.

Acknowledgments

I would like to acknowledge the following people: editors Martin Barnard and Laura Hambly, who so professionally helped to better organize and present my working drafts; Dr. Keith Henschen and Dr. Barry Shultz from the Department of Exercise and Sports Science, University of Utah, for their continuing support, guidance, and constructive criticism relative to my development as a sport scientist; and Dan Mills, Ben Tiffany, and the staff at Mills Publishing for the opportunity to hone my marginal writing skills through my monthly articles in the *Utah Sports Guide.*

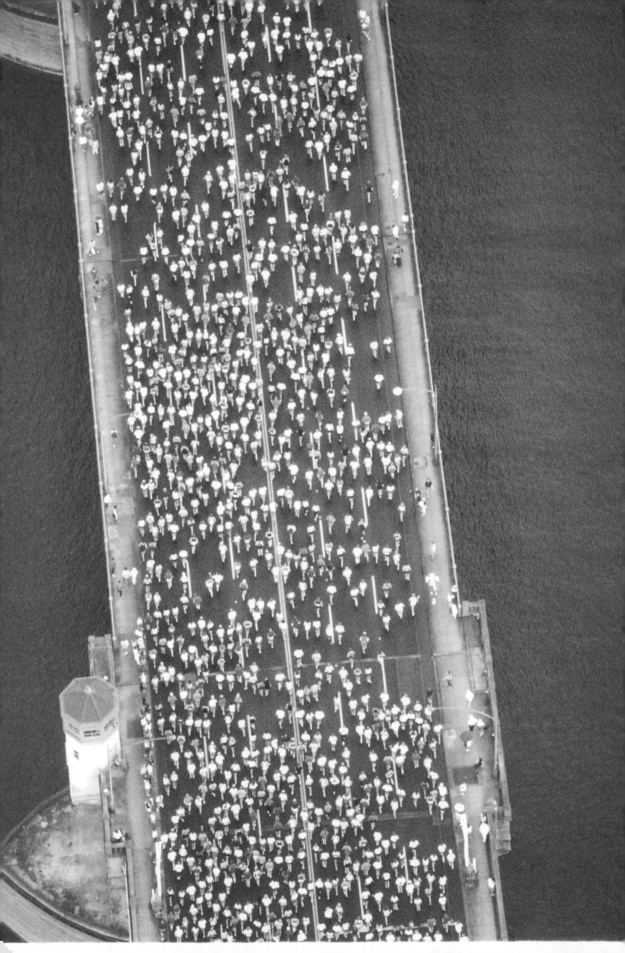

Lessons From a Roads Scholar

This is a love story! I love to run. My passion for running began nearly 40 years ago, and I love to run now more than ever. In junior high school, I desperately wanted to make a sport team, but I thought I wasn't big or skilled enough. When I got up the courage to go out for football in the ninth grade, I played for a coach who made his players run laps as punishment for mistakes they made in practice. By the end of the season, I realized that I would rather run laps than practice football.

I thought about going out for the cross country team in high school, but I didn't want to run for a coach who rode a motor scooter while yelling at his athletes to run faster during hill repeats. Later, when I started Syracuse University with only a vague idea of what I wanted to study, I turned to running on my own to ease the confusion in my life. After a couple of years of college, I decided to join the military—which, indirectly, is what finally spurred me to become serious about running.

The Army, Navy, and Marine Corps recruiters shared a one-room office in Meadville, Pennsylvania. Because I had a couple of years of college education and high scores on screening exams, the Army and Navy recruiters promised me a bright future. After I finished speaking with them, I headed for the Marine recruiter, who had been listening to the others while he did some paper work. Feeling pretty cocky about the positive responses I had just received from the other recruiters, I approached Sergeant Book (some names you never forget) and asked, "What will the Marines promise me if I enlist?" Without looking up, he responded, "I won't promise you anything but a hard time for four years." Then he looked me in the eye and added, "You'll get nothing you don't earn and won't get everything you do. But if you can hack it, you'll get to call yourself a Marine." I enlisted on the spot! When I asked what I should do during the 30 days before I was scheduled to report for boot camp at Parris Island, the good sergeant answered, "Get in shape."

My pre-boot-camp training was simple. Remembering the hill training from high school, I decided repeats would work. There was a hill about a mile from the cabin at Conneaut Lake, where I was living. Every day after work, I jogged over to Iroquois Drive and did hill repeats until I couldn't do any more. After a couple of weeks, I was not only running the hill repeats but also taking the long way to and from the workouts and adding sit-ups and push-ups to the routine.

My simple but effective strategy paid off in boot camp. Because I was short and stocky, the drill instructors (DIs) didn't expect much out of me physically. Before long, however, I excelled during physical training. What my DIs attributed to toughness, I realized was the benefit of getting into shape.

After boot camp, I was sent to Pensacola, Florida, for communications school. Our commanding officer, Captain J.W. Ayers, ran every day at the end of the workday and encouraged us to do the same. Soon I was in the habit and becoming even more fit. Captain Ayers recommended me for the Naval Enlisted Scientific Education Program (NESEP). This program would send me to college, with a full scholarship and regular pay and allowances, to get a degree in math, science, or engineering. Upon graduation, I would be commissioned as a second lieutenant. I suddenly knew what I wanted to do with my professional life—become a leader of Marines.

During my enlisted years, several events stood out. President Kennedy was assassinated while I was in boot camp. The Vietnam War began. The North Koreans captured the USS Pueblo, including two crew members, Sergeants Hammond and Chica, with whom I had served in language school while studying Chinese. I was selected for NESEP and assigned to Marquette University to study civil engineering. I married my sweetheart from Conneaut Lake, Ellie Petruna.

And I ran my first marathon. In November of 1968, I noticed a short article on the upcoming Milwaukee Marathon on December 1. The thought dawned on me that this 26-mile race was longer than the distance across the demilitarized zone in Vietnam. Knowing that I would soon be going to 'Nam, I suddenly decided that completing this race would serve as a kind of insurance policy for my safe return from war. All during the fall I had been running five miles in combat boots and playing handball to prepare for basic infantry training. I reasoned that real running shoes were all I needed for the race. I bought a pair of running shoes—Adidas leather cross countries. I wore them daily for a week, often wetting them down so that they would conform to my feet.

The next Saturday, I set out to run four laps of my regular five-mile course. At first it was incredibly easy, and I floated through the first couple of laps. I stopped briefly at our apartment for a little honey and water after each lap. The last five miles were really tough, however, and I found myself walking each cross street and then running to the next stop sign. Nonetheless, I completed the longest run of my life without blisters or injuries, and I felt confident I could handle the marathon.

Race day dawned misty with a slight drizzle coming off of Lake Michigan. I lined up with about 100 other intrepid runners of all shapes, sizes, and ages. I ran at what I felt was a comfortable pace and settled in with another runner. He asked me if this marathon was my first. I responded that it was and asked whether he had run any others. He smiled and said, "Several." I noticed we were running near the front of a large pack of runners with what looked like high school runners off the front. I asked my companion what I should expect. His answer mystified me: "The race doesn't start until the last six miles." We ran together for about half the race. As the weather deteriorated, he gradually pulled away from me.

After about 18 miles, the course climbed a long hill on an out-and-back section before returning to the finish. I was cold, wet, and already out of gas as I passed the bottom of the hill, where the race would finish. An official was telling runners that they could quit because of the bad weather. For some reason I felt insulted. I had come to run a marathon, and I would finish if I had to crawl in. Honey and water lifted my spirits a little as I drudged up the hill. On the flat out-and-back, I resorted to my run/walk routine. Before long, the race leaders passed me on their way back to the finish line. As I spotted my former running partner, who was now leading the race, I realized how much I had to learn about distance running. Those last miles tested my courage and determination. I finished, not crawling but actually running, thanks to the downhill finish. The agony of those last miles was nothing compared to the pain of walking down steps for the next week. At some point during the recovery week, I vowed to run more marathons but never to feel like that again. I wanted to know the rest of the winner's secrets.

Lesson 1: Elite runners are more biomechanically efficient when they run than their nonelite counterparts.

When I graduated, I traded my sergeant's stripes for a gold bar and reported to Quantico, Virginia, for basic officer training. The good condition that I was in because of my daily running helped me again to excel among my peers. Because we knew that most of us would receive orders for Vietnam, developing and maintaining a high state of physical fitness took on new life-or-death significance. Before leaving for 'Nam, I studied Vietnamese for six weeks and said goodbye to Ellie, who was now eight months pregnant.

I spent a year in Vietnam as an infantry platoon commander. During most of that time, I lived with my Marines in several villages where we provided security, built schools and marketplaces, and protected the villagers from Vietcong and North Vietnamese terrorists. Although I didn't run in Vietnam, I am convinced that my mental and physical health were both sustained by the residual fitness from several years of running.

About halfway through my tour in Vietnam, I met Ellie and Tom Jr. in Hawaii for five days. We were thrilled when, several months later, I received orders to transfer to Camp Smith, Hawaii. It was there that I became a student of running.

As a young stud and combat veteran, I resolved to get a perfect score on the Marine Corps Physical Fitness Test (PFT). To achieve my goal, I would have to perform 20 dead-hang pull-ups, do 80 sit-ups in two minutes, and run three miles in less than 18 minutes. I found that increasing my pull-ups and sit-ups to meet the requirements was far easier than running faster. I had to learn to endure the pain of running harder, or so I thought.

About this time, I began running in local civilian races. Much to my surprise, I couldn't run with these "skinny longhairs." I started to notice that the faster runners didn't run the same way as the rest of us, but I didn't know exactly what they did differently. Next, I met local running coach Johnny Faerber, who introduced me to books by world-class coaches Arthur Lydiard and Percy Cerutty, both of whom thought running form was important. Finally, I marveled at the light, quick, fluid strides that Frank Shorter used to win the Olympic marathon in 1972. One thing was now crystal clear in my mind: elite runners run with greater biomechanical efficiency than nonelite runners.

I set out to learn to run more efficiently. My coach turned out to be the Aiea Heights Loop Trail, which led from Camp Smith, high above Pearl Harbor, down Halawa Heights Road, through the town of Aiea, up Aiea Heights Road to the state park, and through the rainforest back down to the base. I ran this course a couple of times a week. When I started, it took me about an hour and a half. Then, after reading about "belly breathing," I began focusing on exhaling in rhythm with my steps. Soon I was making the climb several minutes faster without feeling nearly as tired. Once on top, I found that if I quickened my turnover and thought, "light and quick, light and quick," I could virtually dance through the rooted, rocky, winding section. Finally, by pushing my chest forward a little and keeping my body perpendicular to the ground, I could blast downhill at full throttle, seemingly running just by swinging my arms close to my chest. On one particularly smooth, gradual downhill section, I imagined myself running like Frank Shorter. Within weeks, my loop times dropped significantly. Nonetheless, I was still having trouble breaking that 18-minute barrier.

As I lined up at the start of the next PFT, I resolved not to kill myself but rather to tuck in behind the faster runners and imitate their technique. At first, I thought their strides were too short

By emulating the technique of elite runners, like 1972 Olympic marathon winner Frank Shorter, you can learn to run more efficiently. Here, Shorter is shown competing in a more recent Masters race.

and their turnover too fast. At the turnaround, however, we were just under nine minutes. I thought about striding it out but decided to stick with what was working. I blew across the finish line well under 18 minutes and maxed my first PFT. I was hooked. I decided then and there that even if I didn't possess the body type of elite runners, I could still develop physical running skills to emulate their natural talent—I would become a running technician.

While I was in Hawaii, I raced regularly at distances up through the marathon. I studied every photo of Frank Shorter and other elite runners in a new little running publication called *Runner's World*. I became a student of running, and my performances improved steadily.

My next duty station was the supply base at Barstow, California. In the late 1970s, California was a runner's paradise. Races were held somewhere every weekend. Why do long runs by myself when I could run on well-supported courses? As I searched for practical ways to improve my running, the road was fairly straightforward, if not always flat and smooth. I learned by trial and success, and I shared what I learned with other runners. I came to believe in the reliability of the technique elements I was teaching.

Lesson 2: All runners can develop mental focusing techniques that improve running efficiency.

During the fall of 1978, I entered four marathons but did not finish any of them. By this time I had run about 40 marathons. I wanted to break three hours and qualify for the Boston Marathon. Most of my previous marathons had been between 3:10 and 3:30. My training plan was simple: I would go out on a sub-three-hour pace and hold it as long as I could.

Finally, in early February 1979, I qualified with a 2:58 in Bakersfield. Then, the first weekend in March, I ran a 2:55 in Los Alamitos. During the last six weeks before Boston, I backed off on the long runs and focused on racing 5Ks and 10Ks. I set personal records (PRs) at both distances, breaking 18 minutes and 37 minutes, respectively. I was ready to run Boston.

Developing a Focus Plan

My seeding put me in the middle of the pack of 6,000 runners. I had never run in such a large race, and the thought of it unnerved me a bit. I needed a race plan that I could focus on. Although I was in the best running shape of my life, based on my recent racing performances, and was my leanest at 147 pounds, I believed that the chances of even breaking three hours were slim because of the huge crowd and slow seeding position. I decided my best strategy was to go with the flow and not fight the crowds. My focus plan was to *race each mile as skillfully and efficiently as I could.*

Psychologically, I was feeling great. I had already accomplished my goal of qualifying, my Marine Corps career was going well, and I was staying in Boston with an old Marine buddy, Jim Harris, whom I hadn't seen in several years. This event was my chance to experience Boston.

Just getting to the starting line in Hopkinton proved to be a challenge. Jim dropped me off a couple of miles from the start and promised to meet me in the hills between miles 16 and 18 with a bottle of defizzed, half-strength Coke. I found my starting area and waited for the gun. The seeded start worked well: it only took just over two minutes for me to cross the starting line. The pace quickly picked up, and I put my body on cruise control. The gentle drop during the first 10 miles allowed me to run easily, without pushing, by letting gravity supply the energy while I provided the technique and imagined myself hang gliding back down the soft, smooth trail to Camp Smith.

Things got tight coming into Wellesley College, where the crowd swelled onto the road, leaving room for race participants to run only two or three abreast. I remember passing Cowman Shirk who was wearing his Buffalo headdress and thinking I must be running well. (In those days miles were not marked on the course, so I didn't know my pace.) Then I passed Sue Peterson and her husband, who are from California. Sue had probably run more sub-three-hour marathons than any other woman—this race was the first and only time I ever passed her. Reasoning that she must be having a bad day, I refocused on my breathing while I climbed the last of Heartbreak Hill. Just before the top, I spotted Jim, guzzled down the Coke, swiped his stocking cap (the 40-degree air was starting to give me chills), and yelled that I would meet him at the finish line—but he'd better hurry!

Overcoming Negative Thoughts

As I rounded the corner by Bill Rogers' running store, I heard the first assurance of "just three more miles to go." Of course, I knew the number of miles remaining was closer to six. I wasn't prepared for the crowds. During the last five miles, we were again funneled into a narrow pathway. The people seemed to

© Victah Sailer

In large races, like the Boston Marathon, distractions are numerous. It's important to utilize mental focusing techniques to maintain efficiency.

be yelling *at* us rather than for us. I was becoming unnerved. My legs lost some spring and my mind began to wander. "I hate this. . . . Why do I keep doing this? . . . Shut up bigmouth—let's see you run. . . . How much farther? . . . I'm dying." Then the defizzed Coke started to kick in, and my blood sugar came back to normal. I said to myself over and over again, "Shut up. Just run. . . . Focus. . . . Breathe, two, three, breathe, two, three. . ." I imagined myself running like Frank, lightly and smoothly, as I counted my exhales every third step.

I kept repeating the words, and soon my rhythm returned. I started passing people as my body took over and my mind became calm. If a spectator interrupted my concentration, if I had to dodge another runner, or if I needed to grab water, I immediately went back to counting. Over and over again, people shouting out time splits or distance would awaken the voice of doubt and worry. Each time I would refocus on breathing, counting, and maintaining form. The closing miles were a blur of counting and running. I crossed the line in 2:51. With the two-minute start handicap subtracted, my actual running time was just under 2:50. Not bad for a middle-aged, squatty body!

It took about a half hour for me to realize how fast I had run a marathon in which I had little expectation of doing well. My strategy had been to go with the flow and experience Boston. I didn't even get reliable splits to gauge my progress, so I just focused on racing each mile skillfully and efficiently. Most of the time, my attention was locked into the moment. If I started to worry or have doubts, I refocused on my running skills.

Soon after the finish, the voice of doubt came back: "If it seemed so easy, think what you could have done if you had really pushed." Interestingly, I have little memory of that voice during the later miles. This postrace criticism sounded like jealousy. My effort, especially in the closing miles, had been extremely intense, but it was not forced by conscious thought. I was releasing energy, not harnessing it. It was as though the voice had given control to another part of my mind and then was envious of the outcome. Boston reinforced another important lesson: nonelite runners can develop mental focusing techniques that produce more efficient running skills, simulating the talents of their more gifted peers. I have dubbed this the "psychomechanics" of efficient running.

Lesson 3: Athletes who understand how the brain works can learn to manage their minds better during competition.

My growing interest in running became a springboard to a new career. In the 1980s, while still on active duty as the Marine officer instructor at the NROTC unit, I became a graduate student in exercise and sport science at the University of Utah. With bachelor's and master's degrees in engineering, I assumed that exercise physiology was a logical field to blend my interests in running, endurance sports, engineering, and science into a new career.

The physiology courses fascinated me, providing a scientific explanation for my practical discoveries. As I learned how to scientifically justify the improved performances of the runners with whom I was working, I resolved to find out more about how the mind could affect performance as well.

My first class in sport psychology was taught by Dr. Keith Henschen. I clearly remember him saying in our first class, "While training is a science, performing is an art." My interpretation of this insight provided a metaphor of my own. If understanding how the machine works was the secret to winning races, then Indianapolis racecar crew chiefs would be drivers—but they're not. Drivers focus on performing skills. I was hooked.

Through Dr. Henschen, I came to appreciate the often contrasting points of view of the exercise physiologist and the sport psychologist. Exercise physiologists can take muscle biopsies, measure oxygen consumption, or look at blood tests, and then generalize the findings across similar groups of people. From this information they can develop and evaluate training effectiveness by measuring changes in assessments. Dealing with the mind is not as easy. First, you can't take brain biopsies. How do you measure what athletes are thinking and how their thoughts affect their performances? The problem is especially difficult because every brain is different, and the neural networking that takes place during learning and development varies with each person.

Dr. Henschen's classes introduced me to the right brain/left brain theory of mental functions. This research gave strong evidence that every person has a "dual brain" made up of right and left hemispheres. Each side performs characteristic functions: the left brain is rational, verbal, and analytical, and the right brain, which controls fine-motor movement (physical skills), is creative, artistic, and intuitive. I immediately recognized the similarity between this theory and my concept of having a "mental team," which had been simmering in the back of my mind ever since my Boston race. Let me explain.

On the flight back to Barstow, I reviewed my training and preparation and concluded that my performance hadn't been an accident. I had been ready physically and mentally to run this race. I was still intrigued, however, with "the voice" that I had pretty well managed to silence throughout the race and the calm, focused, energized finish. Sitting there quietly on the plane, I heard a familiar inner voice interrupt my thoughts. "Of course, it was my planning that made it all possible." At that moment, I understood that my mind could be managed to work like a team. Part of my mental team (my left brain) was responsible for planning, organizing, observing, and analyzing—and criticizing me and my running. The other part (my right brain) took care of the actual running. They couldn't both be in charge at the same time, however. Each had its responsibilities, and I was the one responsible for managing my mental team, not the other way around. I learned that *racing is a process, not a result; focus on the process and the results will come.*

During the following years, as I studied and applied the basic concepts of performance psychology, I found that elite-level athletes on the U.S. cross country, Nordic combined, disabled cross country, and biathlon teams, as well as a slew of champion age-group runners whom I coached, all seemed to benefit significantly from applying this dual-brain paradigm. It gave them a rational way to understand how their brains worked so that they could better manage their thoughts, rather than having their minds manage them.

Liz Sonne provides a perfect example of an athlete who learned to manage her mental team. Liz turned to running in her late thirties as a way to manage the stress of being a doctor's wife, a schoolteacher, and the full-time mother of two high school boys. After following Joe Henderson's training program, which was published in *Runner's World,* she ran her first marathon in 3:20 and found a coach to help her. Although the systematic training unquestionably improved her fitness, strength, and endurance, she dreaded racing because she was "never fast enough." Over the next couple of years she continued to creep closer to the elusive sub-three hours while becoming one of Utah's best master runners at shorter distances. After attending a running clinic that I conducted at a local park, Liz approached me and said, "I've been running for several years now and everyone says I should be able to break three hours in the marathon—and I can't. What's wrong with me?" What was wrong with her was that she had come to identify herself so much with her running results that her own sense of self-worth was tied to her racing results and others' perceptions of her. We discussed the idea that running was something that she did, not a definition of who she was. Instead of using her analytical skills to criticize herself, she needed to apply these capabilities to her mental preparation and strategies.

Liz started running with my group occasionally and enjoyed the relaxed atmosphere, but she was still driven to perform better. I recommended that she stay with her coach, because the nature of the training suited her personality, but that we work together on developing her mental skills programming. She had run the St. George Marathon several times, always coming up just short of her goal, and she felt frustrated. She decided to run Grandma's Marathon in Minnesota, where no one knew her and she would feel no pressure.

To involve her left-brain team member, she studied the course description and map, developed detailed travel and preparation plans, drove the course, refined her strategies, and arrived at the starting line ready to race. Knowing her tendency to get down on herself during races, I made several other suggestions to engage her right-brain partner during the race. First, I advised, "Don't wear a watch." Liz needed to focus her attention on how she was running, not whether she was making the next time split. Second, I suggested, "Smile at every mileage marker." This idea was an experiment to get her to manage everything that came up during the race effectively. Third, I told her, "When your inner critic acts up, sing or count until the next aid station, where you can get your blood sugar back up." Finally, I advised her to refocus on running as skillfully and efficiently as she could every time she caught her mind wandering. Running "miles of smiles," Liz ran the first of many sub-three-hour marathons—and learned that racing was a celebration of her training and a reflection of her preparation, not a test of her self-worth.

Lesson 4: To arrive at the starting line in the proper frame of mind, athletes must understand the conflicting forces that act upon their minds and must know how to manage those forces.

For several years, I had the privilege and challenge of guiding a blind runner, Harry Cordellos. We ran a dozen Marine Corps Marathons and three Double Dipsea Trail Runs together. Our most memorable race, however, was the first World Blind Marathon Championship in the Nike Vancouver International Marathon in British Columbia, Canada. The performance-planning principles we developed to meet this challenge became the basis for my doctoral studies and research.

Early one January, Harry called me in Salt Lake City from his home in San Francisco and said excitedly, "Tom, I've got good news and bad news, and I need your help!" The good news was that the first World Blind Marathon Championship was to be held the first weekend in May in Vancouver, and the best blind runners in the world had been invited. The bad news was that to qualify for financial support from the United States Association of Blind Athletes (USABA), Harry would have to win the National Blind Championship in the Boston Marathon two weeks earlier—even though he was the four-time defending champion. Our challenge was clear, but complicated: how would we each prepare to race two marathons in two weeks?

The previous spring, Harry and I had worked hard to improve his running technique. Because of his tendency to "reach" with his feet to detect obstacles, Harry had been running too upright, shortening his stride and pulling himself down the road—a technique that led to chronically tight hamstrings and frequent injuries. Harry learned to put his feet down underneath him and push off from behind his center of gravity, through his toes, to lengthen his stride and improve his sense of balance. A shorter, more compact arm swing, with his hands held higher and his elbows back, produced a faster turnover rate.

On minimal training, Harry and I had run a 3:20 in November in the Marine Corps Marathon. Between us we had run more than 100 marathons. Now speed, not endurance, was our training objective. To improve our speed over the marathon distance, we decided to race 5Ks and 10Ks between January and April. Harry could get partners for races more easily than for speed work.

Courtesy of Harry Cordellos.

Harry Cordellos, guided by Tom Miller, took first in the 1982 National Blind Championship in the Boston Marathon.

Anytime Harry got a chance to do a long run, he went, regardless of the pace or distance. He also did standing bike intervals at the YMCA once a week. I followed a similar program. By gradually upping our mileage toward 50 miles per week and focusing on the quality of our runs, we felt we could safely improve our speed and maintain our endurance while giving ourselves enough rest and recovery. We planned to cut our training in half the week before Boston, take three days off after the race, and focus on recovering during the days before Vancouver. Because there was no training precedent for racing two marathons so closely together, our goal was to start each race as healthy and rested as possible and see how it turned out.

Dismayed by the USABA's insistence that Harry had to win Boston to earn financial support for Vancouver, I asked Nike for help. The company agreed to sponsor both of us for the World Blind Marathon Championship. The race director also asked us to be the featured speakers for the prerace marathon clinic. The Nike sponsorship meant that we could use the Boston Marathon as a long tempo run and even drop out if we hit the wall. We both had run Boston before, so we knew how to use the first 10 miles of gradual downhill to conserve energy, run within ourselves through the hills, and then focus on running skillfully to the finish.

At Boston we pretty much kept to ourselves, relaxed, and rested. On each of the two days before the race, we ran a couple of miles to stay loose. The day of the race, we got off to a good start and cruised through the early downhill miles. As we hit the Newton Hills, the sun came out and the race heated up. At the 20-mile mark we learned we were leading the blind runners. We focused on staying loose and running smoothly. We crossed the finish line in first place in 3:11, suffering a little from the heat. Because we had focused so effectively on running efficiently, we experienced little stiffness or soreness and even jogged a couple of easy miles the next morning before catching our flights home.

In contrast to the relaxed, confident attitude we took to Boston, we were both nervous and anxious about the world championship. The week or so between races went well, and we were both healthy and reasonably well rested. The race committee had us picked up at the airport and taken to the elite runners' dinner. Harry learned during a TV interview that he was the favorite of the 30 or so fully blind athletes from a dozen different countries. Although he was 45 years old, Harry was by far the most experienced.

We had a couple of days to meet the other competitors and to run several sections of the course. Harry had inspired many of the others to take up running. For years he had been referred to as, "probably the best blind marathoner in the world," and other such accolades. When he spoke with the other runners, they often said things like, "Because of you, I'm a runner. You changed my life. I can't wait to beat you." Harry was becoming a nervous wreck, and I wasn't much better. This event was the most important race of his life. Unlike our calm, businesslike approach for Boston, our mood was something closer to panic. What if we blew it?

In the backs of our minds, both of us were distracted by the fear of failure. Sure, this race was the opportunity of Harry's lifetime, but it could also be a highly visible failure—for both of us. I didn't want to let him down. Prerace anxiety—the fear of what might happen—had a firm grip on both of us. Neither of us had ever been in such a high-profile situation. The press, TV, USABA, our sponsors—all were demanding our attention. We had spent virtually no time developing and refining our strategies for preparing and executing the race itself. Our egos had kidnapped our attention and were driving us both up the wall. It was time to get back to the process of race preparation and planning.

Lesson 5: Proper prior programming promotes "phocused" performances—the six *P*s.

Finally, we got some free time together. First we admitted our mutual worries and anxieties. Then we spent an hour or so developing a detailed game plan that started at that moment and took us through the end of the race. We discussed what we would do until the clinic presentation that evening, exactly what we would talk about at the clinic, and what we would do until we went to sleep. We decided when we would get up the next morning and exactly what our prerace activities would be and why. Finally, we agreed on focus objectives for each section of the race and settled how we would handle things like bathroom stops, cramps, water stops, and low blood sugar. We concluded that if our time was close to three hours, we could live with the results regardless of where we placed. A three-hour marathon would be Harry's fastest in five years and would stretch me to my limits as a guide. Our goal was to *race each mile skillfully and efficiently.*

The clinic went extremely well. Harry shared his race strategy, and I reviewed the elements of efficient running technique while Harry demonstrated the movements. We left feeling good about the presentation and committed to executing our race plan to the best of our abilities. Before going to bed, we again reviewed how we would run the race together. *Focus on the process and the results will come!* We were committed to focusing only on what we could control—how we ran each mile. We were now ready to race: calm, focused, and energized. We had just learned that you must understand the conflicting forces that affect your mind and recognize how to manage those forces to start a race in the proper frame of mind.

We woke up two hours before the race to a chilly, drizzly day—with smiles on our faces. It was our favorite racing weather. Following our game plan, we each took a short, hot, bathtub soak to warm our muscles; stretched; ate a slice of bread with peanut butter and jelly; drank a cup of coffee; went to the bathroom several times; and arrived at the starting line ready to race. Just before the start we each drank a can of defizzed, half-strength Coke.

Bang! We were off and running, focusing immediately on developing a light, quick rhythm. For the first eight miles or so, the only runner we were really aware of was New Zealander Tui Ruppi, who had a reported best time of 2:40. Partway up Pipeline Hill, Tui and his tethered partner blew by us and were soon lost in the crowd. Harry and I continued to run with just our elbows touching, unless we got into heavier traffic. Then I would lightly grab his hand and guide him more firmly until we were clear again. We hit our three-hour-pace splits at both mile 10 and mile 15.

On the out-and-back section from miles 16 to 19, we learned that we were in sixth place. We didn't catch the first of those ahead of us until mile 21. Shortly afterward, we started getting on each other's nerves and knew to take double shots of sports drink at the next aid station to get our blood sugar back up. By mile 25 we had caught everyone except Tui. We got a split of

2:52+. Our chances of breaking three hours, with the long hill to the finish, were not good. I felt Harry ease up and yelled, "This ain't over yet. Swing 'em and breathe. . . . Swing 'em and breathe!" Harry immediately refocused, and we got back into rhythm.

As we started up the final hill, I spotted Tui walking, leaning toward his tethered side. He was obviously in a world of hurt. I told Harry, who started jabbering, "Where? How far? Can we catch

Prerace planning is essential to meeting your goals on race day.

him?" I instantly felt his pace drop as he lost his focus. "Shut up and run. Don't think—RUN!" I yelled. Harry counted his exhales out loud, shouting, "One, two, three, one, two, three, . . . " and we roared up the last section of the hill. We could hear the crowd cheering as we charged toward the finish line. We caught up with Tui at the 26-mile mark. Harry and I were at a full gallop and blew by Tui and his guide like they were standing still. Harry won in 3:00:59 and had the race of his life—and so did I. This race was the most dramatic and satisfying experience in my running career. I had been part of winning a world championship. Thanks, Harry.

My experience with Harry provides a dramatic example of the value of performance programming. There is much more to a performance than just physical preparation. The will to prepare fully to meet *all* the demands of competition is the mark of the consistently successful performer. *Overtrying*—having your ego set goals that your body is not prepared to meet and that your training progress does not support—and race-day surprises are evidence of improper, ineffective preparation and execution strategies.

Summary

We all have references or beliefs that shape our perceptions of how things should be. Each of the five lessons described in this chapter required that I let go of old assumptions and shift to a new running performance paradigm.

Early in my career, I thought that running faster meant learning to run harder—learning to endure the pain. The graceful, light, quick, seemingly effortless stride dynamics that I observed in elite runners challenged my blood-and-guts mentality. My approach was not working, and I realized that it was unrealistic to keep doing the same thing over and over and expect different results.

I studied elite runners and learned that I ran better when I ran "like Frank." I also learned that others ran better, faster, and with fewer injuries when they shifted from the upright, heel-banging, low-arm-swing motor habits characteristic of joggers and learned to imitate the technique of more natural runners. Their thought patterns during runs and races—how, what, and when they thought—significantly affected their results. By systematically preparing to meet the physical, mental, emotional, social, logistical, environmental, and technical demands of specific events, relatively ordinary people could consistently achieve extraordinary athletic results. Athletes who learned to understand the dynamics of performing and the ways their brains functioned benefited in their personal and professional lives as well as in their athletics.

I cannot guarantee that if you become a student of your running, assimilate the information in the following chapters, and develop or refine new running paradigms you will become a world champion. However, you can develop world-class running technique, focusing strategies, and performance programming skills to raise your level of racing performance and your love of running. Remember, I said this was a love story.

2

Stride Mechanics

Have you ever studied *how* you run? Why not? Serious athletes in every other sport constantly work on their sport-specific skills throughout their careers. Why not you? Your current running style is a motor habit based on your innate athleticism, adaptations to your training, compensations for injuries, and responses to the aging process. Just because your current running technique feels natural doesn't mean it's efficient or biomechanically sound.

Imagine the impact of improving your efficiency during each step by just a fraction of a percent, and multiply that fractional improvement times the thousands of steps you take in a run. Suddenly technique training sounds smart, doesn't it?

Although I had been dabbling in running technique for years, I was first inspired to learn more about the scientific basis after reading an article by David Costill and George Branham, entitled "How Clayton Measures Up." The researchers reported the results of physiological testing on long-time marathon world record holder, Derek Clayton. They were surprised to learn that he did not test as high as other elite distance runners in maximum oxygen consumption, long considered a primary predictor of distance running performance. They reached this conclusion:

> The physiological explanation for Derek's success seems to be based upon his tolerance of exhaustive work and an economical running style. At every running speed, he uses less energy than any other runner we have examined. (Costill and Branham)

This last sentence caught my attention because two runners of similar weight running at the same pace require exactly the same amount of energy (kinetic energy = mass/2 × velocity^2). I was disappointed that Costill and Branham did not continue to investigate, identify, and report the characteristics of Clayton's "economical running style." I decided to become a student of running and figure out how to become a more economical runner myself. I concluded that the following factors might contribute to more efficient running styles:

- Elite runners are more relaxed when they run because they waste little effort in nonessential tension and movements (biomechanical skills).
- Elite runners recruit other energy sources to supplement muscular effort (recruitment skills).
- Elite runners breathe more efficiently (breathing skills).

Inspired by the riddle of Clayton's economical running style, I began to research the literature to either prove or disprove my own suppositions and to discover other factors that contribute to running efficiency. My ultimate objective has always been to figure out how to translate this kind of knowledge into more graceful, rhythmic, dynamic running for myself and others. Let's examine what I found on running technique, supplementary energy sources, and breathing skills.

Running Technique

During an 80-day period in 1978, Henry Rono broke four world distance records. When asked to explain the emerging dominance of Kenyan distance runners, especially those from his Rift Valley, Rono responded:

> A young boy from my tribe will copy the style of the adults. If I saw another runner who was better than me now, then I would watch him and see what he was doing and learn what makes him better; I would copy his style. This is the way we are. (Rono 1979, 34)

This chapter takes the same approach. The sequence of photos in figure 2.1 illustrates the running technique of Jim Ryun. Ryun was the first and fastest of only four American high schoolers ever to break the four-minute mile, with a 3:55.3. Although these pictures were taken in the 1970s, they still serve as a valuable tool for observing and analyzing the technique of an elite runner. In fact, studying current videos of scores of Kenyan and other elite African marathoners reveals that their styles are virtually identical to Ryun's. Just as Henry Rono modeled his technique after great Kenyan runners, you can improve your own technique by modeling it after Ryun's. I will refer back to these photos to help illustrate the elements of efficient mechanical technique.

Stride Phases

A runner's stride can be divided into three phases: drive, recovery, and support. The following describes each phase, along with the technique that recent research has proven to promote efficient running.

Drive

In the drive phase, the driving leg thrusts from well behind the runner's center of gravity to power the body forward (see figure 2.1, e–f and k–l). The driving phase ends when the toes of the driving leg leave the ground after the hip, knee, ankle, and toes sequentially extend rearward (see figure 2.1, d–f and j–l).

Recovery

The recovery phase begins as the driving foot leaves the ground and continues until that same foot contacts the ground again (see the right foot in figure 2.1, a–c and f–l). Allowing the knee to bend and the heels to kick up toward the buttocks shortens the lever of the leg. This bent, "short" leg requires less energy and can swing faster than a straighter, "long" leg during the forward leg swing (see figure 2.1, h–j).

a   b   c

right foot recovery   support

g   h   i

right foot recovery   support

FIGURE 2.1 This sequence of legendary miler Jim Ryun serves as a perfect model for efficient mechanical technique. The boxes added to his legs help illustrate the changing positions of the pelvis and femur during Ryun's stride cycle.

d   e   f

j   k   l

Support

The support phase begins as the forward-swinging foot recontacts the ground very close to beneath the runner's center of gravity (see figure 2.1, c and i). Before the foot makes contact, the leg completes its forward swing and begins to swing back, so that the foot is already swinging rearward when it meets the ground (see figure 2.1, b–c and h–i). In the support phase, the foot provides a stationary platform from which the driving forces are launched (see figure 2.1, c–e and i–k).

Stride Length and Frequency

Research conducted by Buckalew et al. (1986) reveals the differences in stride characteristics between faster and slower runners. It further supports the advantages of adopting (and maintaining) the technique that's shown in figure 2.1 and described in the stride phases above. At the 1984 U.S. women's Olympic marathon trials, Buckalew and associates videotaped runners at miles 9, 16, 20, and 24. They were able to identify 40 of the runners at each location. These 40 had an average finish time of 2:37:48. The researchers compared the stride characteristics of the top 10 and bottom 10 finishers in that group.

Early on, both groups of 10 shared similar stride characteristics. At mile 24, both groups maintained similar stride rates (1.53 versus 1.51 strides per second), but there were significant differences in three other measures. The slower group was now running with significantly shorter strides than the faster group (2.36 versus 2.57 meters per stride—a difference of 4 inches per step). The ratio between the time their feet spent on the ground and the time their feet spent in the air was also greater (2.84 versus 2.28)— the faster runners' feet spent less time on the ground and more in the air than the slowing runners' feet. The third measure shed light on both of these findings. To compare percent overstride, Buckalew and associates calculated the ratio between the distance in front of the center of gravity at which the foot struck and the distance behind the center of gravity at which toe-off took place. At mile 24, the respective ratios were 14.1 versus 16.1. In other words, the faster runners' feet contacted the ground more underneath their bodies, while the slowing runners' feet touched the ground more in front. (The faster runners moved more like hang gliders, even when tired, than the slowing runners.)

The researchers concluded that, during the final stages of the race, the faster runners were able to maintain their turnover rates and stride lengths with shorter ground contact and more air time. As the slower runners tired, they straightened up (became more erect or upright) and increased their overstrides by reaching forward, which shortened their strides and increased their ground contact time. Buckalew and associates also reported that the trials winner and Olympic champion, Joan Benoit Samuelson, ran throughout the race with less overstride and shorter ground contact time than the averages of the 40 subjects!

Interestingly, the inefficiencies that the slowing marathon runners demonstrated in the closing miles are similar to the age-related stride characteristics of aging sprinters. Hamilton (1993) found that while stride frequency slows only slightly with age, stride length shortens significantly. Also, the older the runner, the more time each foot likely spends on the ground rather than in the air. Hamilton also found that younger runners toe off after their legs straighten, well behind their centers of gravity, while older runners tend to lift up, with their legs still slightly bent, from more underneath their bodies. Finally, older runners tend to keep their feet much closer to the ground as they swing their legs forward after push-off, while their younger competitors bring their heels up toward their buttocks during the forward swing.

Levering Off

The studies by Buckalew et al. and Hamilton support the importance of pushing off from well behind your center of gravity in the drive phase. Even so, while they suggest that runners concentrate on using their butt muscles and hamstrings to pull the upper leg back into proper position for push-off, I don't. Here's why.

Tight hamstrings are one of the biggest thieves of speed and are almost always associated with overstriding—pulling rather than pushing yourself down the road. To understand this concept better, stand up and take a step forward. Now, with your forward foot flat on the ground, simultaneously pull it backward and reach back with your hand to feel what happens to your hamstrings. They tighten! The same thing happens when you overstride. Hamstrings are not prime movers. Their design is more suited to providing balance and bending the knee when the foot is unweighted. Do not try to contract your hamstrings to pull the upper leg into position for push-off. Focus instead on keeping your foot flat on the ground and letting your forward momentum carry you over it, so that it is behind you before you push off. This approach will automatically align the hip for flight. After you lever off the toes, your heel will automatically swing up toward your butt.

Look carefully at figure 2.1, c through f (pages 26–27). Imagine the changing positions of Ryun's pelvis as he extends to lever off his toes. A rectangular pelvis "box" and femur "bar" have been added to figure 2.1 to make it easier to analyze the relative positions of the pelvis and femur during Ryun's stride cycle. His pelvis demonstrates a degree of flexibility; the driving leg side tilts forward, allowing the hip to extend rearward. This movement is not totally unlike moving forward while balancing a broomstick in your hand. As you would tilt your hand to maintain the balance of the broom as your speed increases, so Ryun's pelvis tilts as he maintains the dynamic balance of his spine and upper body. During recovery, his pelvis approaches vertical. This position allows the foot to contact the ground under his center of gravity and below a slightly bending knee. It also reduces the tendency to reach with the leg.

Noted speed coach Brooks Johnson (1997) also emphasizes the importance of using the foot as a lever to transfer power from the extending leg through the toes and kicking the heel up higher as the leg swings forward to increase both stride length and stride frequency. He counsels runners never to try to lengthen stride by reaching more in front of the body, but rather by pushing off more forcefully.

Johnson's observations are consistent with exercise physiology research, which shows that when elite runners are run to exhaustion on a flat treadmill, their calf muscles, which are utilized during levering off, are the ones that become depleted (Costill 1986). The rate of glycogen depletion becomes more even between the calf and thigh muscles during uphill or downhill running. This study supports Johnson's observation about using the foot as a lever, especially as it relates to track running. I have personally observed that slower runners deplete the muscles in the backs of their legs, limiting their treadmill performances. If hard runs tend to leave you with tight hamstrings, you are too upright, and you pull yourself when you run. If long, gradual, fast downhills leave you with sore calves, you can add another dimension to your running by learning to lever off all the time.

Posture

In *Galloway's Book On Running* (1984), Jeff Galloway devotes a chapter to running form. Most of his recommendations regarding technique are similar to those of other coaches and researchers. As much as I respect and admire Galloway's influence with millions of runners, however, I disagree with his assertion that runners should run with an erect posture. The illustration he identifies as the incorrect, leaning form is identical to that of most Kenyans, while the correct, erect form is similar to that of runners who follow in the Africans' wakes. In addition to my own observations, several other researchers and coaches have challenged the wisdom of teaching upright, erect running.

I like the term *balanced posture,* meaning that the body weight is supported by the skeleton and balanced over the pelvis during movement. To experience balanced posture, stand up straight. Lean first forward and then backward from the ankles and feel the tension that develops. Now seek the posture that relieves the tension you experienced in the leaning positions. Notice that your bones are stacked on top of each other and that your joints are aligned vertically. When you add forward movement, you need to subtly adjust your posture to maintain a balanced position. During leg drive, your body develops a slight lean to align itself with the direction of the driving force (see figure 2.1, e–f, page 27).

George Sheehan once suggested that it is helpful to imagine your upper body as a jockey riding above your hips. A jockey does not sit straight up in the saddle but rather balances his weight lightly over the horse. Like a jockey, you should try to maintain balance and rhythm with your posture and arm swing in such a manner as not to interfere with the natural movements of your lower body. Adjust the balanced forward posture dynamically in response to speed, terrain, and headwind, so that your skeleton rather than your muscles continues to support your bodyweight. If your posture is too vertical, you'll need to use your muscles to keep from falling backward as you step forward, and—to offset the backward movement of your upper body as your lower body is propelled forward—you'll overswing both your arms and your legs in front of your center of gravity, resulting in a heel-first, straight-legged foot contact that sends the impact up through your legs and joints to your spine.

More recently, even Galloway has softened his stand on upright posture, in an article entitled "Easy Glider" in the November 1999 issue of *Runner's World*. In essence, he suggests that runners can maintain or increase running speed with less or equal energy by leaning forward slightly; contacting the ground underneath them with shorter, quicker, strides; and utilizing forward momentum and gravity. He recommends applying the strategies during slight downhills and at the end of races. My question is, why not utilize this balanced forward posture all the time—like the Kenyans do?

Arm Action

The arms and shoulders work with the opposite legs and hips to maintain balance. The upper part of the arm moves relatively straight backward and forward while the lower part of the arm may move slightly across the body during the forward swing (see figure 2.1, a and f, pages 26–27). The hands should be carried in a relaxed, cupped position and held fairly close to the chest, at about heart height, to reduce the blood-pumping effort to the arms.

Since arm and leg movements tend to mimic each other, you can help control the tempo of your run by focusing on your arm swing. In "Running Economy, Anthropometric Dimensions, and Kinematic Variables," Owen Anderson observes, "Quick, little arm movements—in synchrony with the swing of the legs—are the ones that produce the most economical running" (1994a).

Recently, Craig Poole and I were discussing the Ryun photos. Craig, who is head coach of the women's track team at Brigham Young University, pointed to parts e and k in figure 2.1 (page 27) and noted how important it is for distance runners to allow that heel to rotate up toward the buttocks and then swing forward with the recovering foot pointed downward at knee height. Craig also noted that Ryun's elegant extension as he toes off (in figure 2.1, f and l, page 27) is initiated by driving the opposite elbow back. In fact, during the later laps of high schooler Alan Webb's sub-four-minute mile in the New Balance Games in January 2001, his coach Scott Raczko "implored him to 'Keep going! Drive your elbows back!'" (Bloom 2001). Craig pointed out that both turnover and push-off are managed by posture and arm swing. This observation comes from a coach who routinely takes walk-ons and turns them into all-Americans. He went on to say not only that running technique is the foundation of performance but also that it can be taught and learned.

Foot Plant

You should make foot contact with a relatively flat foot (see figure 2.1, c and i, page 26) and then roll forward over the ball of the foot toward toe-off. The foot should strike the ground after it has completed its forward swing and is swinging rearward (see figure 2.1h, page 26). It should make contact directly under the slightly bent knee (see figure 2.1, c and i, page 26).

Lift one foot up and let it relax while suspended. Note the slight inward cant of the foot. Johnson (1997) says that the natural foot plant should start with contact by the outside part of the foot, just behind the little toe, and then roll inward as the foot flattens. This limited pronation and flattening of the arch is the natural shock absorber in the foot. A heel-first contact requires a straightened leg and sends the shock upward through the body, so that any structural weakness in the major joints or back absorbs the shock. Thus, a heel-first landing is not recommended.

Elements of Efficient Running

Here are the key mechanical elements of efficient running technique:

- Initiate foot contact after the recovering leg has completed its forward swing and has begun to swing back under the body. Your feet will mimic the forward swing of your hands. To reduce overstriding, don't let your hands swing out in front of your body. (see figure 2.1, c and i, page 26).

- Land nearly flat-footed underneath a slightly bent knee (see figure 2.1, c and i).

- While you swing your upper arm back and up, bringing your hand to just above waist level at your side, let forward momentum carry your upper body over and beyond your foot so that your hip and upper leg extend rearward behind your center of gravity (see figure 2.1, d–e and j–k, page 27).

- Let your backward-swinging upper arm lift your shoulder slightly, thrusting your chest forward and aligning your upper body as, in sequence, your hip fully extends, your knee straightens, your ankle rotates, and your foot levers off through the toes (see figure 2.1, f and l, page 27).

- During recovery, kick up the heel of your trailing leg toward your butt as your shoulder drops; swing your arm forward with your elbow bending slightly; and keep your hand close to the body as it goes from your side, just above the waist band, to heart height (see figure 2.1, g–l, pages 26–27).

- Run with a compact arm swing, with your hands close to your chest (see figure 2.1; b, f, h, and l, pages 26–27).

The Leaning Towers of Kenya

"Sammy Kipkiter just hit the first mile in 3:59!" gasped the P.A. announcer at the 2001 Carlsbad 5000 elite road race in southern California. An electric charge surged through me and the other spectators near the 2.5-mile mark. We soon heard, "8:11 at two miles!" I steadied my trusty old Nikon set on continuous-shutter mode and, knowing that I had driven a thousand miles for these next few seconds, stared nervously through the viewfinder. I could hear the crowd's roar approaching, and then, suddenly, Sammy flitted by to the six-frames-per-second clicking of the camera. Then, with my heart racing and hands shaking, I was clumsily reloading—racing

Sammy as he returned from the turn-around. "Here he comes. Got 'em. Gotta reload for the women!" In a heartbeat the women, who had started five minutes behind the men, were on us, and chaos erupted again.

Sammy tied his world road record of 13 minutes flat and led eight other Kenyans to dominate the men's race completely. The Kenyan women, paced by Sally Barsosio's winning time of 15:20, also ran impressively. Let's analyze my photos to see if we can detect running technique differences that may contribute to the success of "Air Kenyan" runners. Then we'll discuss how to apply that knowledge.

FIGURE 2.2   Kenya's Sammy Kipkiter. Notice his forward balanced posture.

FIGURE 2.3   Mexico's Teodoro Vega. His upright posture is less efficient than Kipkiter's forward lean.

As I've already suggested, the photos were taken under less-than-ideal conditions, but you can still get a sense of the speed, grace, and fluidity of Sammy's technique. The most striking element of his biomechanics, which was also demonstrated by the other Kenyans, is the balanced forward posture that he maintains throughout his gait cycle. Figure 2.2 dramatically reinforces this postural observation—Sammy's shoulders are always in front of his hips as he extends his forward movement by lightly falling forward. You get the sense that his legs are spinning behind him, with toe-offs well behind his center of gravity, high heel kick-ups to shorten his legs and increase his turnover rate (requiring less energy during recovery), and instantaneous foot contact. Contrast the Kenyan posture, leaning forward from the ankles, with the classical technique of Mexico's Teodoro Vega in figure 2.3. Teodoro's upright, nearly vertical posture is consistent with the recommendations of most traditional experts. He is, however, trailing eight Kenyans who are all "leaners." Teodoro's arm swing appears more compact and efficient than Sammy's. Nonetheless, Sammy covered more ground in the time my automatic-shutter mode took to fire the three photos of each. Even through the viewfinder, I recognized the quickness of the Kenyans' foot strikes and the efficiency of their movement. Their forward lean was just enough to use gravity to extend their forward momentum a little more per step than did the upright postures maintained by those who followed.

FIGURE 2.4   Kenya's Sally Barsosio. Notice the compact arm swing and forward lean.

FIGURE 2.5   Japan's Noriko Takahashi. Her upright posture and long, low arm swings reduce her efficiency.

Figure 2.4 shows Sally Barsosio powering toward the finish line. Rather than *striding out*—reaching forward with her legs and taking bigger arm swings as most less knowledgeable runners tend to do—she is exaggerating her short arm swing to increase her turnover rate while maintaining the same stride length. I also noted this subtle arm-swing adjustment in the Kenyan men as they pushed to the finish. Again, the Kenyan lean is apparent. Contrast Sally's technique with that of Noriko Takahashi of Japan, who came by nearly a minute later (see figure 2.5). Noriko's upright style robs her of forward momentum, and her less efficient, long, low arm swings not only take more energy but also contribute to her postural

(continued)

inefficiency. She appears to reach and pull herself down the road. Because she runs with great leg speed, my advice to her would be to adjust her posture and arm swing so that her legs do their work behind her more than under her.

The fact that all the frontrunners in this world-class race demonstrated similar technique characteristics—especially balanced forward postures and quick foot strikes—is strong evidence that these elements are critical to the Kenyans' efficient running technique. To get a sense of the advantages of these elements, stand up at attention with your arms at your sides. Now lean forward from your ankles while keeping your body straight. Feel yourself being drawn effortlessly forward—gravity is doing the work. Now stand up straight again, but this time only on one foot. Maintaining your vertical posture, hop forward quickly and monitor the effort it takes. Now try hopping again, but this time first lean forward from your ankle to initiate the first hop, and maintain the lean as you lightly hop forward. The leaning hops take less energy, but more quickness, than the upright hops, because plyometric (elastic) energy assists the muscles during push-off and gravity extends your momentum. The

leaning hopping drill mimics the instant foot strikes of the Kenyans. Incorporate hop-like foot strikes with the Kenyan lean. Play with it during your running, but be prepared to run like the Kenyans—*faster!*

Finally, to prove that even nonelite runners (normal people with jobs and families) can learn to run more efficiently, I submit for evidence the following sets of photos taken during a video session shortly after I returned from Carlsbad. The first sequence is of Tom Jow, a 38-year-old assistant manager at the Wild Rose Bike Shop, cyclist, Nordic and telemark skier, and really cool dude. Tom began running with my group a year or so ago to keep in shape for his other sports. He has never run a race. When he started with us, he ran uphills like a duck on steroids—he had incredible power but was grossly inefficient. He's corrected his splay-footed foot contact by thinking "pigeon-toed" and learned to stop running with "chicken-wing" arm swings. The results are shown in figure 2.6.

In the evening session, ultradistance runner Debbie Moss and local speedster Mike Evans asked to be videotaped. Debbie, a full-time mom, wife, and nurse, has learned the value of efficient tech-

FIGURE 2.6   Tom Jow emulates the technique of elite runners.

FIGURE 2.7   Ultradistance runner Debbie Moss.

nique in 100-milers, and one of her secrets of success is knowing exactly what to focus on to maintain efficiency. Figure 2.7 demonstrates her skills.

As fast as Mike is, he's always looking to shave seconds. Through the video, he observed that his asymmetrical arm swings were costing him time, effort, and speed. Figure 2.8 captures what he observed. Notice how low his left hand is in the first photo and how far back his left arm swings. The second photo shows him just a fraction further through his gait cycle as he pushes off with his left leg. Notice that his right arm is carried higher and more compactly during this drive phase than his left arm was in the previous photo. The third photo shows the consequences of this "minor" flaw: he tends to overreach with his right leg and contact the ground farther in front of his body. This more straight-legged contact and the associated impact forces explain his frequent injuries to that leg. Mike's arm swing dictates his turnover rate, not the other way around. His "longer" left arm takes longer to swing back and forth than his "shorter" right arm. His turnover rate, therefore, is controlled by his slower-swinging left arm. As he practices symmetry of arm swing, he'll gain a couple of steps more per minute at his normal stride length—which means he'll run faster.

What I hope you have gleaned from this photo-essay is that although we can't all be born in Kenya or have great natural talents, by studying the biomechanics of how super-runners run we can develop physical and mental running skills to simulate their talents. When you become a student of your running, you will run better, have fewer injuries, train more consistently, and race faster—which is always a blast!

FIGURE 2.8   Photos help runners like Mike Evans identify and correct minor flaws, like the asymmetrical arm swing shown here.

Supplementary Energy Sources

These analytical, objective descriptions show the elements of efficient running technique, but they still don't account for why natural athletes run with the light, quick, fluid stride dynamics so characteristic of elite runners. Let me explain.

In 1972, I had the opportunity to run in the Amateur Athletic Union National Marathon Championship in northern California (not because I was fast, but because I paid the entry fee). The route was a five-lap course, and my goal was not to get lapped by the leaders. At about mile 22 or 23, I was chugging along when I heard the pitter-patter of little feet coming up behind me. The winner, Doug Schmenk, went by me so effortlessly that I looked down to see if my feet were still moving. I still have a vivid memory of his weightless, quick, flowing steps as he danced away from me. Although he was some 35 pounds lighter than me, I resolved to learn someday to run like him. Now, nearly 30 years later, I can run like him—just not as fast. My secret is to use the natural elasticity of my leg muscles to complement muscle contraction.

In the 1999 article titled "Moving Up," David Kuehls discusses body type and running style. The article quotes Frank Shorter: "You simply have to be light on your feet. It's called the friction coefficient—how heavily you come down when you run. It doesn't matter if you're big or small as long as you're light on your feet." (90–91) I couldn't have said it better myself. So, how do you learn to be "light on your feet"?

Most biomechanical literature centers on providing efficient power through economy of leg movement. When we watch elite runners, however, we are most impressed with the fluid gracefulness of their movements, not their power. None of the coaches or researchers discuss the light, rhythmic, almost dance-like grace of the gifted runner. I have some ideas about where they find this extra energy.

Stand up, hold your toes up, and jump up and down. Feels awkward, doesn't it? Now jump up and down normally. Notice how your knees and ankles bend slightly and how the muscles in your butt, thighs, and calves stretch on impact. As you spring upward, the elastic component of the stretched muscles releases and assists the muscle contraction. Feel the lightness and quickness in these "assisted" jumps. The muscles that stretch as the hips, knees, and ankles flex are releasing *plyometric energy*.

According to Jack Wilmore and David Costill (1999, 104), ". . . plyometrics uses the stretch reflex to facilitate recruitment of additional motor units. It also loads both the elastic and contractile components of the muscle." Elite runners more effectively tap into this energy source, which in turn contributes to their light, quick, fluid movements.

Let's continue our plyometric experiment. Play with the following sequence of actions while studying the Ryun photo sequence on pages 26–27:

1. Start walking with a little bounce in your step, and experiment with changing your foot contact from heel-first to flat-footed (see figure 2.1, c and i).

2. Next, extend your hip to the rear so that your thigh starts rotating further behind you. Notice that your downward bounce has moved back a bit, to a point more under your center of gravity. Feel your knee rotate behind you, and sense your hip flexors stretch (see figure 2.1, d and j).

3. Feel your toes bend and then straighten as you push off (see figure 2.1, e and k).

4. Time your toe-off so that it triggers your spring forward (see figure 2.1, e and k).

5. Finally, make a point of toeing off until you feel yourself falling gently forward, with little sense of effort (see figure 2.1, f and l).

Repeat these steps until you feel your body respond to each adjustment as your pace quickens.

The next phase is to adjust your posture and arm swing. Once you can quickly get into the rhythm from the waist down, shift your attention to your upper body. Try this experiment:

1. As you start to extend your leg rearward to push off, simultaneously swing your upper arm straight back, a little farther than normal, as though you were going to put your hand into a rear pocket. Be sure *not* to lift and hold your shoulders up as you do this. Feel your chest thrust forward as your arm reaches back (see figure 2.1, d–f and j–l).

2. Adjust your arm swing so that your hand swings from heart height, with your wrist just touching the side of your chest, down to just above your waistband at your side. Your elbow

should unbend a little on the downswing and bend a little on the upswing (see figure 2.1, f–j).

Keep playing with these adjustments until you can quickly get into a light, rhythmic, flowing stride pattern. Welcome to the wonderful world of coordinated, harmonic movement! It should now seem plausible that economical running uses plyometric energy to assist the driving legs. Photos d and j in figure 2.1 (page 27) catch Ryun in his down bounce, which loads the legs for his spring forward, depicted in photos e through f and k through l. Using this energy is how most of the Kenyans fly, and you can too! Now let's look at turbo-charging your hang gliding.

Breathing Skills

One morning, after waking up to the smell of pine needles and the freshness that only a midnight thunderstorm in Montana can bring, I left the nearly 70-year-old log cabin where I was staying on Hebgen Lake, near West Yellowstone, and chugged up the one-lane dirt road on my way to Trapper's Creek. The magnificent mountains and sparkling blue sky were inspiring, but my quads and glutes reminded me that I had rowed my canoe several times during the last couple of days, and they were tired! For a brief moment, I thought about bagging the run and jogging back for a swim. Then I decided to refocus on quick, sharp exhales in rhythm with my shortened strides, and for the next 45 minutes I continued climbing up the long switchbacks until I was at the end of the road, high above the lake. I smiled because I knew what was next—hang gliding home on the perfect downgrade of the logging road, followed by a swim and a cold soak in the lake.

Nearly 30 years earlier, I had learned my lesson from the Aiea Heights Loop Trail in Hawaii. Climbing is primarily about strength and power, but you can only climb as hard and fast as your breathing will support. Downhill running is primarily about technique, focusing on posture to maintain momentum and on breathing and arm swing to sustain rhythm. Flying down the logging road was like traveling through a time tunnel—I was young, quick, and strong, blasting down through the rainforest to Camp Smith. My 57-year-old body celebrated the run back to the cabin and eagerly looked forward to the dive into the cold mountain lake.

Focused Breathing

When I ask my runners which skills or concepts benefit them the most, the majority respond, "rhino breathing"—purposeful concentration on exhaling rhythmically in step with running. Breathing is the natural focus objective for most forms of meditation, and running, at its best, is a form of dynamic meditation. You can only run as fast and hard as your breathing will support, but *how* you breathe is the key.

While in the last 30-plus years running publications have virtually ignored the topic of breathing, *Sports Illustrated* published an article titled "The Secrets of Speed" while I was still in Hawaii. The only new revelation for me was about breathing. Bowerman and Brown (1971) suggested that breathing should be steady and rhythmic. They recommended learning to exhale in patterns that coincide with foot strikes, and they suggested puffing the cheeks just before exhaling to enhance carbon dioxide/oxygen exchange in the lungs.

Because most of my daily runs from Camp Smith involved hills, I had a great opportunity to test this new style of breathing. I soon found that focusing on my breathing made me feel more centered during my runs. I learned to do puffing exhales by contracting my stomach muscles sharply while pursing my lips. To inhale, I only had to relax my stomach muscles, and air was sucked into the vacuum. On hills, I found myself grunting rhythmically every other time my left foot struck the ground. (Since I was in the military, the left-foot grunt was automatic.) I found it helpful, however, to switch regularly to exhaling when the other foot struck. Within a few weeks, I was climbing Aiea Heights Road several minutes faster than ever before. I developed a variety of puffing patterns to use under different circumstances. When I was warming up at the start of a run, I would inhale for a couple of steps and then exhale for a couple of steps. On uphills, or when I was running faster, I sustained my efforts with short, harder, one-step exhales followed by a couple of steps of inhales.

Belly Breathing

As I started sharing my breathing techniques with other runners, I noticed that novice, bigger, and older runners seemed to benefit more than well-trained, lightweight runners. I also noted that most of us had developed the habit of chest breathing—sucking air into the chest. Stand in front of a mirror and inhale deeply. If your chest extends and your shoulders lift, you are breathing backward. The stomach muscles are the most powerful breathing muscles under stress. As you inhale, you should inflate your belly. Watch small children or animals inflating and deflating as they breathe—this method is the natural, most efficient way to breathe. As we grow up and become image conscious, most of us develop the habit of "holding it in," resulting in less efficient chest breathing. Watch how you belly breathe when you are relaxing in a comfortable easy chair, and then observe the shift to chest breathing as you stand up. To learn to belly breathe, "squeeze" the air out of your body by contracting your stomach muscles. Pretend you are squeezing the air out of a ball with your fingers at the same time. This strategy has worked for many of my runners. If you purse your lips and puff your cheeks just before you exhale, you'll feel your stomach muscles contract.

While I was studying for my master's degree, I had a conversation with Dr. David Costill that helped me understand why belly breathing helped some runners more than others. According to Costill, running at a given pace takes the same amount of oxygen per unit of muscle mass per minute regardless of the total mass of the runner. In other words, because I use more muscle mass at a given pace than my skinnier peers use, I have to consume and process more air than they do. Later, I learned that carbon dioxide is some 20 times more soluble in the lungs than oxygen. If the carbon dioxide is not exhaled, some of it will be reabsorbed into the blood stream instead of oxygen and will adhere to the hemoglobin. By sharply exhaling "old" air, therefore, you allow "new" air to be absorbed more easily. Moreover, carbon dioxide that is not expelled breaks down and may hasten the buildup of lactic acid from lactates. Although rhino breathing helps older athletes, heavier and more muscled runners, former smokers, novices, and less fit runners more than lightweight, small-framed, naturally gifted runners, even the elite can benefit from learning to focus on their breathing and biomechanics during the later stages of races.

The next opportunity you have to watch a roadrace, observe the breathing techniques of the frontrunners, the midpackers, and the tail-enders as they near the finish line. Typically, the leaders breathe with short, forceful exhales and quiet inhales. The midpackers begin to gasp as they start their drive to the finish. These runners suck in harder as they try to breathe more deeply.

All runners, even the elite, benefit from learning to focus on their breathing and biomechanics during the later stages of races.

© Victah Sailer

Finally, the slowest runners often don't change their effort or breathing at all.

When I first observed that faster runners tended to emphasize their exhales as they increased their efforts, I began to teach runners to belly breathe. Later, I found research that supported my supposition. Bramble and Carrier (1983) observed that the higher the performance levels of runners, the greater the tendency to exhale rhythmically, in synchronicity with their foot steps.

Finally, during my own doctoral research, I administered standing, high cadence/intensity bike interval training to two groups of matched, experienced runners. I taught breathing skills to one group of runners, however, as part of training on focusing strategies, while the other group did only physical training. Post-training testing results showed that although both of the groups had similar physiological characteristics, the "breathers" stayed on the treadmill longer and improved more in the 10K time trials than did their peers. In other words, their focus on their breathing helped them become more efficient than the runners who focused on effort instead. The breathers learned to anticipate increases in workload (beginnings of intervals, increases in elevation on the treadmill, uphills, and time-trial finishes) and to increase their exhaling intensity just before they felt the increase in workload. They learned that although they could only run as fast as their breathing would support, by focusing on their exhales they could sustain their speed longer, slowing less in the final stages of the time trials.

Not everyone agrees with my conclusions about breathing. The most common argument is that you don't see the Africans "huffing and puffing." I agree, you don't, but that doesn't mean that they are not exhaling rhythmically. Also, keep in mind that the average elite male marathoner is something like 5'6" tall and weighs between 118 and 123 pounds. The average elite female marathoner is about 5'3" and 100 pounds or less. Their lung capacities are probably equal to those of larger runners, but because they are diminutive in stature compared to most of us, the amount of oxygen they need and the amount of carbon dioxide they must exhale may be less at a given pace. I do know that developing breathing skills has been helpful for the vast majority of runners with whom I have had the privilege of working.

Regardless of a runner's level, body type, or size, focusing on breathing is always useful during the latter miles of marathons. After about two hours of fairly intense racing effort, most of us have pretty well exhausted our glycogen energy supplies. Elite racers are toughing out the last mile or so while the rest of us may still have a long way to go. Once you use up your glycogen stores, you are forced to slow down because your body has to switch to fat metabolism to keep moving. This form of metabolism requires more oxygen but gives off little carbon dioxide, so that your respiratory center is not signaled to increase your breathing. Therefore, focusing on your breathing will allow you to slow down less and help you maintain your rhythm.

While I maintain that you should focus primarily on exhaling, there is an exception to this rule: altitude. At higher elevations, where the oxygen concentration is significantly thinner, two-way breathing is essential. You can remain relatively efficient in your movements, but everything will be slower. Hang in there. Do you know how long it takes to feel better when you start back down from the summit in the Pikes Peak Marathon? About three steps! Now it's time to learn to fly.

Summary

Efficient technique is the foundation on which your running and racing performance is based. It is also the most ignored aspect of running by athletes at all levels. Most elite American runners are not at the same level as elite Africans because their running techniques are not as efficient. Runners at every level can benefit by learning and internalizing the elements of efficient running technique.

Similarly, regardless of your running level, you can lighten your foot strikes by developing stride dynamics that employ an element of plyometrically produced energy. Combining more efficient technique and plyometric foot strikes will reduce injury, promote consistent training, and enhance your racing performance and running enjoyment.

Finally, developing and refining breathing skills will allow you to manage your efforts more effectively throughout your runs. A natural focus of attention, effective breathing emphasizes a sharp exhale produced by contracting stomach muscles. This technique allows you to run at higher intensities longer. You can only run as fast as your breathing will support. Enhancing your breathing efficiency raises your redline—you can run faster longer.

Now that you understand the elements of efficient biomechanics, let's learn how to implement these principles when you run.

3

Psychomechanics

One of the basic tenets of performance psychology is that superior performers use more effective focusing strategies than do athletes who are equally gifted physically but less successful. The following discussion is based on research and years of observing and interviewing elite athletes to find out what they do with their minds so that their bodies can perform their best.

Gaining an intellectual understanding of efficient running mechanics is a necessary step in the process of improving your running style. The essential step, however, is wanting to improve how you run and committing yourself to reaching that goal. Without this commitment, your mind will continually come up with reasons not to change, such as "This feels weird," "This is too hard to do all the time," "The old way feels more natural," "So-and-so doesn't run like this," etc. Remember, your current running style is a product of your innate athleticism and your adaptations to your past training, compensations for injuries, and aging. It's just a motor habit! Why not make it a better habit? Analyzing and refining sport-specific technique is the mark of professional athletes—it's how they get better. Why continue training to run inefficiently?

Psychomechanics is the art of programming your mind to direct your physical movements accurately. In other words, what, when, and how you are thinking at any moment influences how you are running at that moment. For example, what comes to mind when you hear, "This hill has no end," "I'm running out of gas," "This is stupid, why do I keep doing this?" and other similar complaints? Disaster—what you focus on will happen. It's up to you to take charge of your mind and tell it when to either shut up or work with you. You first have to take responsibility for your thoughts and direct your mind to assist you in this adventure. Instruct your mind to become a partner instead of a critic, and you will be surprised at the insights that will come to you. In this chapter, you'll learn how to

- assess your current running style;
- develop an array of psychomechanical skills to reprogram your guidance and control systems for more efficient running technique;
- apply psychomechanical skills to run faster and more easily; and
- train for improved speed, power, and endurance.

Assessing Your Technique

Watching yourself run, preferably on video with slow motion, is the single best way to determine if you want to change how you run. Video is the great lie detector that allows you to reconcile your perception of how you run to the reality of how you actually run. If you don't have access to video, run past windows and observe your reflection, check your shadow, or have a running partner mimic your running style. Relying on how you think you are running or having someone else critique your style is less effective.

Common Inefficiencies

Look for these common inefficiencies:

- Movement is stiff and mechanical rather than coordinated, rhythmic, and fluid.
- Hands/feet swing too far in front of the body, forcing the posture to be too erect and rigid rather than balanced and relaxed.
- Foot contact is heel first, with a straight leg in front of the center of gravity, instead of nearly flat-footed, beneath a slightly bent knee nearly under the body.
- Elbows stick out to the sides (chicken winging) or are locked at a 90-degree angle, so that the shoulders swing the arms rather than letting the bending elbow assist the arm swing.
- Hands/feet swing too low, with limited elbow bend and heel kick-up.
- Upper arm/upper leg doesn't swing back far enough to cock the upper body for flight, thrust the chest forward to extend momentum, and position the straightening leg to release maximum energy from the toe-off.
- Movement is powered by "reaching and pulling" instead of "loading and firing."

Effective Focus Objectives

You should also look for positive elements. Do you run with fluid, rhythmic movements as shown in figure 3.1? Are you maintaining a dynamic, balanced forward posture? Here is a short summary of effective focus objectives:

- Refine the positions of your hands, arms, elbows, and posture, and your foot placement and leg drive will automatically improve as well.
- Keep your hands within chest-touching distance as they swing from heart height to just above your waistline, with the elbows unbending slightly, and then back up to heart height. (See figure 3.1.)

- You should *not* be able to see your hands on the forward swing.
- Keeping your forearm at heart height, reach back with your upper arm (figure 3.1b), to cock your shoulder and thrust your chest forward, properly aligning your body to release energy more effectively during leg drive.

So far this discussion has been aimed at your left-brain programmer—the intellectual, analytical part of your brain. The trick now is to get that side of your brain to share information effectively with the right side, which actually controls fine-motor movement and learns through repetition, intuition, and imagery.

a   b   c

d   e   f

FIGURE 3.1   This sequence of Sheryl Harper, two-time winner of the St. George Marathon, illustrates the fluid, rhythmic technique and mechanical efficiency that you should look for in your own running style.

Developing Psychomechanical Skills

Assuming that you are now committed to reprogramming your mind and body to run more lightly, quickly, and rhythmically, what do you do next? In this section we will explore visualization/imagery, "audiogenics" (positive self-talk), and a few nontraditional training methods designed to let runners feel and experience efficient technique.

Visualization

When I first became a student of running, I did several things. First I studied the observations of the experts on just what the elements of efficient running were. Then I observed runners at all levels to see if elite runners really ran as the experts described and to understand how their techniques differed from those of less talented runners. Finally, I tried to imitate the techniques of those more talented than me by visualizing efficient form while I was running. I had only limited success, however, until I started playing with dolls and drawing stick figures.

The other night on the phone, my now-thirty-year-old son reminded me that, when he was little, I was always borrowing his G.I. Joe dolls and heading for the bathtub, with the dolls in one hand and a *Runner's World* magazine in the other. The memory of his decorated Marine captain father sitting in the bathtub making Joe run like the elites still makes him laugh. The time I spent posing those anatomically correct, articulated dolls proved valuable, however, as I struggled to understand why the biomechanically gifted were better runners. I became so obsessed that I also took to drawing running stick figures in my free time. One thing became obvious in both these pursuits: if the form looked right, it was right. Soon I had burned into my memory the images of many runners and stick figures—all running efficiently. One of the most effective visualizing techniques I have found, then or now, is to imagine the stick figure running while I am running. When I focus on "running with my skeleton" (with stick figures as a reference), I more accurately communicate to my body exactly what I want it to do. In fact, during the months that I have been writing this book, my own running has regained lost form and speed as I have begun again to use this forgotten technique. Once you can successfully visualize effective technique, imagine yourself in the shoes of an elite runner and "feel" what it is like to run like the elites. In each sequence of the Ryun photos in figure 3.2, pose yourself and get a kinesthetic sense of executing the movements. Feel the forward momentum; experience the down bounce, with your butt, thigh, and calves loading elastic energy; drive your elbows back to feel your upper body wanting to go forward; and extend off your toes well behind your body to feel the energy being released through your legs. Totally experience your running movements so that you can verbally describe every element of running gracefully, lightly, and energetically down the road.

Instead of trying to remember every detail of efficient running style simultaneously, learn to focus sequentially on the elements of each phase of the flight cycle. Study each of these elements until you have a clear image of exactly how it looks and feels. (See figure 3.2.) Repeat the descriptive words over and over until you automatically associate the words and images:

- **Loading**—A relatively flat foot contacts the ground under the body, below a slightly bent knee, as forward momentum carries the body over the foot and, for an instant, the knee bends slightly more, loading the thigh and calf muscles with stretch reflex and plyometric energy (figure 3.2a–b).

- **Firing**—The shoulder has been cocked by swinging the upper arm backward, aligning the upper body with the driving leg. With the pelvis tilted forward and the hip extended rearward, the knee straightens, the ankle snaps, and energies are released through toe-off well behind the center of gravity (figure 3.2c–d).

- **Flying**—With the leading hand close to the forward-thrust chest and with the trailing heel kicking up toward the butt, the aligned upper body glides through the air, using momentum and gravity to maximize the horizontal component of forward motion (figure 3.2e–f).

The key to reprogramming for light, dynamic, fluid flight cycles is to time the cocking of the upper arm and the chest thrust so that they extend the forward momentum provided by the release of the plyometric and muscle-contractile energies in the legs.

a b c

d e f

FIGURE 3.2   Study the phases of the flight cycle to get a clear image of exactly how each phase should look and feel.

Audiogenics

Audiogenics is a term I use to describe image-enhancing words you say to yourself as you run. The words *loading, firing, flying, light, quick, rhythmic, gliding, floating, fluid, striding, smooth,* and *forward* from the preceding pages are positive examples of audiogenic words that stimulate a visual image of Ryun running. As you continue to use them while you train for flight, you will also begin to associate these words with how it feels to run this way. You can literally talk yourself into running better on a bad day by the choice of words you use to talk to yourself. What words describe what you are experiencing during a good run? Add those words to your audiogenics vocabulary.

Imagery goes beyond visualizing a still or moving picture in your mind's eye. It employs as many of your senses as possible to experience more realistically what you are imagining. For example, get in a relaxed position (my favorite place to do mental rehearsals is in a hot, soothing bath with my earphones on). Start by half-closing your eyes and visualizing the pictures of Ryun running. Now get into his shoes and feel what it's like to run with the wind in your face; the sweat on your brow; the instantaneous tensing and releasing of energy in your quads and calves as your foot contacts and then snaps off the ground; and your upper body floating quietly over your legs and then thrusting forward in sync with the firing-off from your toes to create a sense of hang gliding. Be apprehended by your sense of rhythm, grace, and power. The more often you practice using audiogenics and experiencing the images they inspire, the more often you will, in fact, run with rhythm, grace, and power.

This morning, I used all of these mental skills to transform a slow, sluggish, heavy-legged run into a series of touch-and-goes that left me exhilarated and energized nearly an hour later. A couple of days ago, I returned from five days of serious road cycling in the Rockies. Yesterday, I mountain-biked a little and then spent most of the day at my computer, writing. This morning, I woke up feeling a little brain-dead and decided to blow the carbon out with a run. I started off running slowly and felt awkward. On the gentle uphill, I focused on my breathing to get into a rhythm. "In, in, in, out, out, out, . . ." I repeated to myself. By the time I got to the first stoplight, I was feeling a little more energized. I stretched my hamstrings, quads, and hip flexors for a couple minutes and then started across the street for another block. Remembering how good cycling down in my drop bars felt when I was climbing steep hills, I imagined myself on my bike and felt my pelvis tip forward a little. Immediately I sensed my feet landing more underneath me, my elbows swinging back, and my chest thrusting forward. I could feel my leg muscles load and fire as I bounced down and sprang forward. I ran "with my skeleton" by visualizing a stick figure running with perfect form. For the next several flat blocks, I let my body run at its own pace. I started back up a gradual uphill. My breathing became a little more pronounced as the workload increased. I picked up the tempo of my breathing with shorter, sharper exhales to keep my legs light and quick. On these longer blocks, I imagined a rope tow running parallel to the ground and lightly hooked through my belly button and onto the back of my pelvic girdle. As the workload increased, the tow rope pulled me forward by increasing the forward tilt of my pelvis, which in turn put my feet down more quickly but allowed me to push off from farther behind. In my mind's eye, I saw Ryun's elegant compact arm swing and long "hind legs." Soon I was flying from stoplight to stoplight. I finished the run totally pumped and loose. In fact, by running so efficiently, I was much more flexible after the run than before. I still love running!

Nontraditional Training Methods

Olle Larson is the director of the Rowmark Ski Academy, which has influenced many world-class skiers. Olle is known for his nontraditional but unquestionably effective methods for improving ski racing technique. If skiers keep their feet too close together, he has them ski with thick, doughnut-like bumpers around their ankles. He has an array of devices designed to let athletes feel and experience efficient technique. I borrowed this approach recently while doing a series of video clinics.

Swing-Rite Harness

If after reading chapter 2 you tried to apply everything you read, you no doubt couldn't remember all the concepts, much less apply them. I have the same problem when I teach in video clinics. Recently I discovered a quicker method of refining upper body movements than the hours of videotaping I used to do. Try to

Poetry in Motion

Early on in my running career, I recognized the advantages of focusing on image-enhancing words. Out of that fascination came running poems, or ditties—series of connected words that, when repeated in sequence, direct your body to run efficiently. When I first started identifying how it felt to be in the zone, I came up with the poem in the shaded box below. (Move your feet in place and repeat the words under the L [left] and R [right] as the respective foot strikes the ground).

You can experience the effect by tapping your feet (left, right, left, right, . . .) as you repeat the words to yourself. Next, memorize the phrases, and then repeat them as you run. A curious thing often happens. If you are not running as the phrases direct, you will have trouble remembering the next phrase. Once you correct the inefficiency, your memory returns. I also like "Load, trigger (reach back), fire, fly" as a ditty. In this series of words, your focus shifts from lower body (load) to upper body (trigger) to lower body (fire) and back to upper body (fly). Whatever words promote good form for you will work. I sometimes use "Tilt for speed, tilt for speed" to focus on getting a more pronounced forward tilt of my pelvic girdle so that my feet land more underneath me and my push-off is farther behind, which helps me develop and maintain speed more efficiently. Experiment and find what works for you.

"Touch down soft- ly,
L   R   L   R
(Make foot contact under a bending knee)

Float over gent- ly
L   R   L   R
(Don't pull yourself, but let your forward momentum carry you over your feet)

Reach back,
L   R
(Reach back with your elbows to thrust your chest forward and align your body for toe-off)

Extend off,
L   R
(Push off from well behind your body)

Fly,   fly,   fly."
L   R   L

---

find a 54-inch long and one-half-inch wide length of sewing elastic. (I have found these in the sewing section of the local grocery store.) First, tie the ends together to form a single loop. With the knot in the center, make one loop knot in each end for your thumbs. Put one arm through the big loop as though you were sticking your arm into a sleeve. Next, pull the elastic behind your neck and stick your other arm through the other end of the large loop. Now you should have a thumb loop near each armpit, part of the elastic band behind your neck, and part behind your back. (See figure 3.3.) Insert your thumbs into the loops.

Now, with your thumbs in the harness, mimic Ryun's arm swings as shown in the pictures in figure 2.1 (pages 26–27). Doing this in front of a mirror will significantly improve the accuracy of your movements. Keep practicing the correct swing until you feel minimal elastic stretch throughout the range of motion. Notice that as you pull your shoulders back by reaching back with the upper arm, the swing starts to feel more normal. Be aware that as your upper arms reach back, your chest automatically thrusts forward a bit, initiating forward movement. Finally, start to bounce lightly up and down in rhythm with your arm swings. Feel the rhythm! Partially close your eyes and "run like Ryun." Frequently check your arm swing in the mirror until it's perfect. Continue to swing your arms and, with your eyes closed, feel the perfect arm swing, down bounce, elbow cock, and chest thrust. Exaggerate your movements until you feel yourself trying to fall forward. Now try running.

As you start to run gently with the harness, notice when you feel pressure on your neck and back, and adjust your arm swing so that it diminishes. Feel the vertical cord stretch slightly on the downswing as your upper arm swings back and up (the motion feels like reaching back to put your hand in your back pocket) and your hand swings down toward the midline at your side, just above your waistband. Feel the tension in the cord at your back and neck if you reach too far in front of your body on the forward swing or too far below your waistline on the downswing. As you are moving, you should experience the feeling of falling gently forward. If not, focus on pushing your chest forward as your upper arm swings straight back and up. Feeling yourself falling forward means that your posture is extending your forward momentum and gravity is working with you, not against you.

FIGURE 3.3   Running with arms in an elastic harness allows runners to feel and experience efficient upper body technique.

Stride-Rite Scooter

After you become accustomed to running with the harness (and not fighting it), you can add the next step, becoming more aware of your foot and leg movements. Stand up and take a normal walking stride, stopping when your foot first contacts the ground. Typically, you will have contacted with your heel at the end of a nearly straight leg. The ankle is cocked and the toes are up. Hold this position and shift your weight back and forth, testing for stability. The round heel is not very stable. Now, while looking straight ahead, slowly pull your foot back and let it flatten until it feels stable. When it feels most stable, look down at your foot. Most likely, it will be pretty much under your body. Put weight on it. Now bounce up and down lightly, feeling the muscles in your butt, thighs, and calves stretch and load plyometric energy. Take some walking steps, landing in this stable foot position. Just after foot contact, allow your body to drop slightly for an instant, as the body is moving over the foot. Remember the toes-up jumping drill in chapter 2 (page 38), where you learned to jump naturally with a relaxed foot and "load" the muscles. Sense your pelvic girdle tipping forward and your hip extending rearward. Allow yourself to be slightly swaybacked rather than ramrod straight and upright. Be aware of your knee swinging behind your center of gravity just before your leg straightens and you toe off. Feel your body spring forward as the stretch reflex assists the extension of the leg and toe-off. Continue experimenting with the timing of the release of plyometric and contractile energies.

Often I run into stubborn "heel bangers" who just can't seem to break the habit of landing heel first. Here is where the Stride-Rite Scooter comes in. Look closely at the photos of Joann Garuccio, five-time World Masters Triathlon Champion, as she pushes off on a scooter (see figure 3.4). Notice the similarity between her running and scootering foot contacts and toe-offs. Scootering allows heel bangers to experience what it feels like to push off from well behind the center of gravity. Moreover, those who land heel first while on the scooter immediately feel the impact slamming up through their extended forward legs as they jerk awkwardly along. Within a few steps they learn to impact with their feet already swinging rearward, and soon they are smoothly maintaining their momentum. Within a few minutes, the placement of their foot contact adjusts and begins to feel natural. As soon as I see this happening, I immediately have them run while imitating the scootering leg movements. The transformation is often spectacular.

I regularly train with my scooter for several reasons. First, it effectively reinforces stride technique. Second, research has shown that running leg strength can increase faster when the strength training mimics the running motion, and the scooter works the legs at or near the same speed as running, one leg at a time. This fact makes scootering uphill intervals a killer strength workout. I also work on leg speed on the scooter on the flats. Because I only go one leg at a time, I can actually work at a much higher turnover rate per leg, while maintaining a slightly exaggerated but effective range of motion. For more information on training with scooters, go to my webpage at **www.scooterbikerun.com**.

a   b   c

d   e   f

FIGURE 3.4   Training with a scooter helps get rid of bad habits by reinforcing efficient stride technique.

Running Faster and More Easily

Watching the decathletes and running event specialists at the last Olympics, I was struck by the contrast in the effort they displayed in the final stages of their respective races. The decathletes grimaced and strained to get every last ounce of energy out of their bodies while running down the home stretch. Their heads came back, their arms tensed and swung in big arcs, and their faces became strained and distorted as they gave their all.

The winning event specialists, on the other hand, tended to become more fluid and relaxed, with faces flaccid and expressionless but arms, legs, and upper bodies moving in perfect harmony with each other—unforced effort. The specialists were able to focus their energies from only those muscles actively required to move them down the track. The decathletes were giving 110 percent; none of the tensed muscles in their faces, necks, or hands were connected to their feet—the only place force could be applied against the ground. This misplaced effort caused them to run more slowly than the more relaxed specialists, who were running with very little wasted effort or motion. Running faster means learning to relax the muscles more efficiently, not just running harder.

To illustrate this last point about "easy speed," flex your bicep with your elbow bent 90 degrees. Now tense the whole arm, making a tight fist, and then shake your fist back and forth as fast as you can while maintaining tension throughout your arm. Shake your arm out and resume the flexed position again, but this time relax your arm and shake your hand back and forth. Feel how much faster it goes. "Fast, relaxed, fast, relaxed" is an effective exhaling mantra when you sense yourself tightening up.

Speed Play Versus Speed Work

I have always disliked speed work. The hard efforts followed by recoveries that were too short always left me stiff and sore. During the last 30-plus years of my running career, I have diligently avoided track intervals. I found them boring, hard, injury-inducing work. I preferred to get my speed from hills, short races, time trials, standing bike intervals—almost anything but track intervals. Recently, however, I have grown to look forward to "playing" on the track. The measured oval has become my group's experimental "landing strip," where we develop psycho-mechanical skills to run faster, farther, and more easily by practicing "touch-and-goes."

I have finally realized that right from the beginning I always associated speed work with just that—work! Learning to run faster meant learning to run harder. Look at almost anything written about training. It's usually centered on adapting to ever-higher levels of work. Members of my running group have often found an interesting contradiction in our fastest races, however—almost all of them felt easy, like we were on automatic pilot for most of the race.

In my group, we have recently changed our attitude about track workouts because we are having more fun running faster. Playing harder is much more fun than working harder. Our speed play has a two-fold purpose:

1. To discover, develop, and refine focus strategies to improve biomechanics, attention-focusing skills, and economy of effort and movement
2. To develop a keen sense of pace and form during increasing levels of effort and fatigue

Developing, refining, and applying better psychomechanical skills is a habit well worth enhancing. You run the way you do now out of habit. Your technique feels normal and natural because you are used to it, not because it is inherently right. Applying psychomechanical skills initially helps you learn how efficient form feels. By conscientiously focusing on improving your style for three to six weeks, you will reprogram your neural muscular movement patterns. Additionally, you will change your audiogenics from things like "Push it, push it, harder, harder," which invoke tension, to words like "Faster, faster, smoother, smoother, flow, flow, flow," which promote light, quick, graceful movements.

Also, you will learn what to focus on in the harder stages of workouts and races to maintain form and pace for an optimum performance. You will become a predator of speed. Your hunting skills are attentional focus, economy of effort, and stride management. Like the Indy 500 race car drivers, you will learn to maintain speed not by chasing the clock (Indy cars have no speedometers) but by instantly and accurately responding to your bio-feedback (other gauges) with subtle changes in posture, arm swing, stride dynamics, and breathing.

Allow yourself to become one with your running during those moments when you integrate body, mind, and spirit. You are not proving your courage or toughness but experiencing the joy of becoming one with yourself through your running. Remember, *running is a process. Focus on the process and the results will come.*

Speed Play Formulas

Speed play is not limited to running in circles on the track. It can, and should, be done anywhere, anytime, and it can be structured or spontaneous. Its form is only limited by the size of your imagination. The secret is to have a very clear image in your mind's eye—both a picture/movie/video and the kinesthetic (body feedback) cues associated with running with perfect form. Another important ingredient is to run repeats instead of intervals. The difference is that the objective of intervals is to build aerobic power by reducing the rest between work sessions. In repeats, the objectives are to teach the body to run with perfect form and to become accustomed to faster paces. Longer rest periods during repeats allow you to maintain the quality of your workout throughout the entire session. Remind yourself of the purposes of your "psycho" repeats (mental training objectives to be accomplished during each repeat) before you take the first step during each running session.

Warm up with a light, quick turnover. Feel the muscles in your quads and calves loading up and firing off through your toes. Feel your toes bending just before you lightly snap your ankles and toe off. Feel your heels bouncing up behind you. Fall gently forward from your toe-off. Extend your momentum by driving your upper arms back and up, thrusting your chest forward so that your body floats lightly over your feet. Enjoy the light rhythm and soft down bounce and forward springing steps. Exhale rhythmically with your steps. Try breathing in for two or three steps and out for two or three steps. Get in touch with your body—listen carefully, for it only whispers, unlike your ego, which loves to yell.

Once you break a light sweat, stretch a little, paying attention to your hamstrings, quads, calves, hip flexors, Achilles, back, and shoulders. Then repeat the warm-up process (preflighting) and get ready to do "touch-and-goes" (repeats). Running the straights and recovering on the corners is a great way to introduce yourself to this type of reprogramming. I am partial to 400s.

Regardless of whether you do a structured speed play with set intervals, run the blocks and walk the cross streets, run a set number of minutes with recoveries, or run at a steady tempo, the preflight process is the same:

1. Focus your mind on what you want your body to do.
2. Warm your muscles and get into the mood.
3. Stretch your muscles, joints, and connective tissue.
4. Let go of your inhibitions and allow yourself to play—fast!

For an easy speed play, go to the track and warm up, stretch, and do your preflight. Say you decide to do quarters. Until you have been doing speed play for several weeks, I recommend you leave your stop watch at home. You need to learn to focus exclusively on how you are running and what allows you to run more gracefully and efficiently. Before you start your lap, run lightly and quickly in place. Rev up your engines. Check your systems. Feel your shoulders rise and drop as you swing your upper arms straight back and forth. Be aware of your hands staying close to your chest (you should not be able to see your hands on the forward swing when you're looking ahead) as they swing from just above your waistband at your side to heart height. Use the Swing-Rite Harness. Feel the loading of your leg muscles. Start rhythmic, patterned breathing, puffing your cheeks slightly before each exhale. Now thrust your chest forward and take off the brakes. Feel yourself hang gliding after toe-off, your upper body floating above the ground. Play with your posture and with timing your arm swing with the release of loaded and contractile energies in your legs. Let your movements apprehend your attention as you build speed. Run at a steady, controlled effort while seeking to optimize your posture, arm swing, and stride dynamics to gain the easiest speed possible. Activate cruise control/autopilot. Observe the flight. Become your running!

Toward the finish of a race, notice how the leaders increase their turnover rate, not stride length, to improve their speed and sail to the finish.

Improving Speed, Power, and Endurance

Why do we want to run faster? Because, as Frank Shorter once put it, "Running fast is more fun than running slow." From a mechanical standpoint, to run faster you have to be able to increase your stride frequency, stride length, or some combination of both for a given distance. In other words, you have to conduct training designed to increase your leg speed and strength, and you have to learn to apply these components in the most efficient manner. An incredible number of athletes don't have a definitive answer when I ask, "Exactly what is the objective of your race training?" They typically say something like, "Learning to run harder longer." Sound familiar?

Research shows that elite distance runners, male and female, tend to run at 180 steps per minute. Reviewing video of the diminutive African runners suggests that they run at an even faster turnover rate. The next time you see a big race on TV, try mimicking the leader's arm swing to get a sense of how fast that really is. Obviously, when you train to improve your speed, one place to look is your turnover rate. Go for a run and count your steps per minute. I typically check my counting, "zero, one, two, three, . . ." for 10 seconds and then multiply by six to get an estimate. I once calculated the relative advantages of increasing my turnover rate by 10 steps per minute without changing my stride length versus holding my stride frequency constant and adding an inch to each step. Increasing stride frequency gained me about 30 seconds per mile, whereas increasing stride length gained me only 10 seconds per mile. Toward the finish of a race, most people think, "Stride out," when they should be thinking, "Spin 'em."

A recent article in *Scientific American* addressed the issue of how running training will change in the future to ensure continued improvements (Schechter 1999). In the article, Michael Yessis, an emeritus professor of sport science at California State University at Fullerton, answered that until now most runners have been running with genetically endowed abilities. In the future, these talents will be enhanced by "more scientific methods," which will include "strength training that duplicates what [the athletes] are doing in their running events as well as plyometrics, a technique pioneered in the former Soviet Union." The following innovative approaches to speed, power, and endurance reflect these "more scientific methods."

Speed Training

Back in the 1960s and 70s, one of the revelations coming out of the communist bloc was the use of downhill training for runners. With gravity providing an energy assist, communist athletes learned to run faster downhill than they could on the track. Because they increased their leg-speed capability, however, their track times got faster as well. Track intervals primarily build leg speed, not strength or power, because the workload only changes with speed. Downhill training accelerates the adaptation process. In either case, your primary focus cues should be body posture and short arm swings. I use the rope tow image on the track to direct my body to tilt my pelvic girdle more and put my feet more underneath me. Then, with a solid, balanced forward posture that has me falling gently forward, I shift my focus to a compact, quick arm swing. Your turnover rate is dictated not by your leg turnover but by your arm swing, which connects to your legs by the *crossed extensor reflex.* In other words, focus on your arms to increase your leg turnover. Leg speed and stride frequency are only half of the equation, however. The other half is leg strength and stride length.

Power Training

Recent *overspeed* training for distance runners, developed by Dr. Jim Walker at the Orthopedic Specialty Hospital in Salt Lake City, has been getting startling results. The training involves short intervals on a very steep treadmill at faster than race pace. The principle is that motor learning transfers from fast to slower movements, but not from slow to faster ones. Dr. Walker's runners do several uphill, hard, fast repeats followed by flat intervals, also done at a pace that is faster than the runners' current race pace. By doing the uphill intervals, the runners also build strength and power through a greater range of motion and at faster stride frequency than they could on a flat track. The additional motor units that fired on the uphills continue to fire on the flat intervals, resulting in more speed and power.

Finnish researchers recently published findings that validate Dr. Walker's overspeed training concepts and that can serve as a base for other forms of innovative training (Paavolainen et al. 1999). In their study, "Explosive Strength Training Improves 5-Km Running Time by Improving Running Economy and Muscle Power," the researchers divided 18 experienced, highly fit runners of similar ages into two matched groups. The subjects had been running about 75 miles per week, with a traditional ratio of distance, speed, and strength training. The volume group continued this training. The explosive group reduced their volume of training to about 50 miles per week and, in sessions totaling about three hours per week, conducted a variety of short sprints, plyometric jumps with and without weights, and rapid weight training with ranges of movement similar to running. Both groups were given the normal physiological testing and raced 5K time trials before and after the nine-week treatment period. The researchers also collected data on stride lengths and time of foot contact.

The volume group showed significant increases in both maximum oxygen consumption and lactate thresholds, which meant they could work longer and harder than they had before. The explosive group didn't show any improvement in those measures. Typically, researchers end their analysis here: because the measures went up with volume training, it was more effective. On the other hand, the time trials and speeds that each group ran at thresholds contained some puzzling results. Although the volume group's measurements went up, the speeds that the subjects ran to reach the thresholds did not go up, nor did their 5K times improve. In other words, after nine weeks of high-volume training, they could run harder but not faster. Members of the explosive group, however, were now able to run significantly faster at their old thresholds and averaged nearly 30 seconds faster in the second time trial. Further analysis revealed that the volume group now had longer foot-contact times than the explosive group, which maintained the same stride length, but with shorter contact time—a faster turnover rate. They were running more quickly with the same aerobic horsepower as before. Where did the additional energy come from? It stemmed from the elasticity that their muscles developed during the sprinting and plyometric training. As this study exemplifies, the more distance training you do, the higher the probability that you will lose overall speed when you do distance training at the expense of sprinting/plyometric training.

My friends and I have developed a workout that applies the motor learning and adaptation principles of both overspeed and explosiveness training. We call it the "Avenues" workout. The Avenues is an old residential area in the foothills of Salt Lake City. From 1st to 18th Avenues are uphill blocks. After a 10-minute warm-up, we start at the city cemetery at 4th Avenue and run straight up to 5th Avenue as fast as we can without losing form. We jog slowly on the flat until we're fully recovered and then blast up the next block and repeat the process until we've had enough—usually to 12th Avenue. Then we jog slowly down to 11th Avenue, fly on the flat for one block, continue running down to 10th Avenue, and reverse directions, still running fast. Because the muscles are so used to the uphill demand, the flats feel incredibly easy and fast. After each "U-fly," we totally recover before beginning the next set of U-flies. The idea is to maintain the highest quality of running during the ups and U-repeats.

This workout accomplishes several things. Not only do my friends and I practice running faster and harder on the uphills (building strength and power) but we also learn to maintain fast running (enhancing leg speed) when we're tired on the flats and downhills by focusing on technique. On the uphills, I exaggerate my balanced forward posture and imagine myself climbing on a bike, standing up, well forward of my feet. I focus on driving my knees behind me, using my quads to straighten my legs, and toeing off to fire me up the hills. On the flats and downhills, I focus on "spinning" by swinging my arms quickly while maintaining overall good form. As I tire, I objectively observe how long I can maintain my speed primarily through arm swing and forward posture. This killer workout should not be done more than once a week and not more than two or three weeks in a row—max! The payoff comes in the form of better stride dynamics through reduced overstriding, faster turnover rates, shorter foot-contact times, and slightly longer stride lengths—faster running and more fun.

Bike and Psych Interval Training

For my dissertation research, I chose to study the effects of cycling cross-training and performance programming on matched groups of experienced runners. I conducted a 10K time trial first and, based on the results, divided the subjects into two matched groups. The subjects ranged from 18 to 63 years old and included both men and women. All participants were also tested in the lab, with the normal array of physiological assessments. The groups proved to be similar based on the testing and time-trial results. The respective individual and group pre-treatment results then served as baselines with which to compare post-treatment results.

For six weeks following the initial time trial and physiological testing, all subjects had to agree to maintain their current levels of training and not to conduct any speed-work training or participate in any races. Instead of speed work, each group met once a week for bike intervals with me. The bike group received only bike interval training, while the psych group received mental skills instruction in addition to the interval training.

The interval training consisted of a 10-minute warm-up followed by standing work intervals of 30 seconds, 30 seconds, 45 seconds, 45 seconds, 60 seconds, 60 seconds, 45 seconds, 45 seconds, 30 seconds, and 30 seconds. Each work interval was pedaled as close to 90 RPMs as possible and against the greatest resistance the subjects could handle. During the 60-second recovery between intervals, subjects were encouraged to spin at 90 RPMs or faster.

The psych group received additional instruction while pedaling. First, they were informed that the lengths of the work intervals coincided with the lengths of the repeated climbs in the four-lap, rolling, 10K time-trial course. Then, they were encouraged to imagine themselves running these uphills during the bike intervals. The recovery spins were similar to the short downhills on the course. Again, they imagined themselves spinning down the hills on foot. They learned to focus on their exhaling and pick up the intensity of their breathing just before the work intervals started, instead of waiting until they were gasping for air. They were taught to emphasize their exhales in rhythm with their pedal strokes. They watched videos of elite runners and imagined themselves running in the elites' shoes. Finally, they mentally rehearsed the post-treatment 10K while conducting their last interval workout. After each session, the psych group received relaxation training before going home, during which they were reminded what they had learned that day and were told that they would sleep soundly and wake up refreshed.

The final time-trial results were startling. The psych group's average 10K time improved 11.69 percent (from 50.20 minutes to 44.41 minutes). This change was practically and statistically better than the bike group's, where the average 10K time improved 8.57 percent (from 47.15 minutes to 43.11 minutes). Of the original 12 men and 10 women who volunteered as subjects, 11 male and 8 female runners completed the training and testing programs. Two of the faster psych-group runners and one of the slower bike-group runners had to drop out due to injury (not related to training) or personal/work conflicts, creating a disparity in the average time-trial times between the two groups. However, since each individual was also his or her own control group (just as in the real world, where you measure your improvement over previous performances), the performance gains were indeed exceptional.

In fact, 17 of the 19 subjects recorded all time PRs for a rolling loop course.

As expected, while the psych group did make greater performance gains in the final 10K than did the bike group, there were no statistical differences in the results of their post-treatment physiological testing. This evidence strongly supports the performance-enhancing attributes of psychomechanical skills training and performance programming.

Sadly, I didn't have the foresight to videotape the 10K so that I could analyze any changes in stride dynamics that might have resulted from the training. Nonetheless, because the subjects, like the Finnish runners, stayed on the treadmill significantly longer to reach their initial threshold levels after the training, some implicit evidence suggests that these changes were similar to those found in the explosive training research group. The testing protocol requires the runners to run for given periods of time at increasing inclines and speeds. Because they stayed on longer during the post-training testing, the speeds and inclines had to be greater than when they were first tested. Moreover, the nature of uphill running on a treadmill precludes overstriding so that, to perform longer on the treadmill, the subjects also had to shorten their foot-contact times and increase both their turnover rates and the explosiveness of their push-offs. These adaptations are the same ones that both the Finnish researchers and Dr. Walker observed in their runners.

Endurance Training

The "more mileage" trap is common among those of us who started out jogging for fitness. At first, we didn't like 5Ks because they hurt and weren't fun. Eventually we moved to the marathon, where just finishing was enough to inspire the respect of our nonrunning friends. We found that as we ran more miles, we got faster in races. This phenomenon can go on for several years—especially if you were really slow when you started. But sooner or later you have to face the fact that long, slow training and racing develops long, slow runners. The more distance training you do, the more speed you will lose, unless you adjust your training to include intensity. Most people realize this, but they are reluctant to reduce volume to do it. This big mistake typically leads first to nagging little injuries and frequent illness and then to serious chronic injury.

The secret is figuring out what is enough speed, power, and distance training to meet your racing goals. I can't answer that question for you. However, here are some guidelines to help you develop your training:

- Although you will probably do your long runs at slower than race pace, practice your race turnover (with shorter strides) during these extended runs. Condition your muscles to move at the quicker tempo so that come race day all you add is a little more push-off. Adrenaline will provide it initially, and your intelligent taper will have left your muscles loaded and ready for running.

- If you are relatively new to running, longer runs will stimulate the development of blood vessels in the heart and muscles ("plumbing"), so longer runs are essential at any speed. If you've been running for years, your plumbing is in place and you need to tune up your blood pump by increasing heart stroke volume through intensity of training.

- If you are preparing for a marathon, at least the last half of each long training run should be at or faster than the pace you want to race.

- If you want to increase the pace of your races, the best predictor of results is your average training pace. If your average training pace improves, so will your race times. As a rule, your collapse point at your current average training pace is three times the length of your average daily run (not counting days off) over the last two months. This formula means that for a marathon you should average between eight and nine miles per run over two months (prior to tapering). Remember that a 15- to 20-miler every other week allows for lower mileage during the week. Also consider a 5K or 10K race in between long paced runs.

- Long runs promote blood volume that you can literally idle away during your taper before a long race if you don't include some intensity during the lower-volume period before the race.

When a group of high school runners asked Doug Padilla what secret allowed him to run at the world-class level for 10 years, he replied, "The volume of training you can sustain is based solely on the amount of time you have to sleep." Therefore if you are running 50 miles per week and sleeping eight hours, don't try to go to 75 miles per week unless you can increase your sleep proportionately to 12 hours. Most of us don't have the luxury of that much free time. Find out how much sleep you need to recover within 48 hours of hard or long training runs or races, and stick with it. Quality of runs is much more important than quantity. Too many long runs break you down and suck away your speed.

Training Menu

Developing a variety of training alternatives is important to prevent overuse injuries and maintain motivation. Be sure to analyze your training needs and then develop methods that will meet those needs. Here are some options.

Traditional Methods

- Steep uphill repeats emphasizing explosive push-off and proper arm swing
- Uphill repeats focusing on form and quickness
- Gentle downhill repeats with a faster-than-normal turnover rate
- Flat intervals on a track, focusing on body posture and efficient arm/leg swing
- Fartlek speed play on roads or trails, focusing on lightness, quickness, and form
- Tempo runs at 75 to 90 percent of race effort for one-third to one-half of the race distance
- Sanity runs (easy pace, any distance) to burn off stress-induced hormones
- Sightseeing runs
- "Yak attack" runs to catch up on the news and gossip with friends
- Thinking runs to sort out problems (Define the problem before starting. Focus on form. Allow your subconscious to sort through the issues and let them pop into your head. Repeat the solutions several times before returning your focus to the run. Otherwise, you will often forget these incredible revelations.)

Sightseeing runs are a great way to vary your training and maintain motivation.

Nontraditional Methods

- Standing, high-resistance (forces you to stand up), high-cadence (approaching 90 RPMs) bike intervals of 30 to 60 seconds' duration with one-minute recoveries (Imagine yourself running uphill with perfect form during the standing segments. Feel yourself levering off your toes at the bottom of the pedal stroke. Shift your weight slightly over downward stroking pedal. Don't use toe clips or step-in pedals. Spin the recoveries.)

- Seated, high-cadence bike intervals (100 RPMs or faster for one to five minutes' duration—position the seat as high and forward as required to simulate running posture)

- Running against a stretch cord attached at one end at ground level and at the other to a belt or, better yet, a shoulder harness

- High step-ups with a hop (Using a knee-high bench, step up on the bench with one foot and hop straight up and down with the same foot, and then step back down with the opposite foot. Change feet and repeat. This exercise builds great leg strength because your range of motion and workload is greater than in flat or hill running.)

- One-leg squats, jump rope, and hops for leg strength and plyometric training

- One-leg hops up stairs (great for identifying leg strength differences and then strengthening the weaker leg)

- Cross-country and roller skiing, classic technique (great for refining kinesthetic awareness, balance, and overall conditioning)

- Scootering or skateboarding uphill (Because the push-off position of the feet is exaggerated well behind the body and the resistance is greater than in running, these exercises build leg strength that translates into stride length. Imagining skateboarding or scootering while you run is also effective.)

You'll also want to develop a repertoire of images to visualize while you run. Here are some to choose from.

Psychomechanical Imaging

- The push-off from a skateboard or scooter
- Your upper body like a jockey riding the lower body—position and movements of torso and arms all contribute to forward movement
- The roadrunner cartoon character—wheels spinning behind balanced forward upper body
- Hang gliding—floating over the ground, not pounding on it
- A puppeteer lifting you uphill with strings attached to your elbows
- A rope tow enhancing your forward pelvic tilt during speed work and racing
- A deer running—light, rhythmic, forward bounding

Focus on reducing internal resistance to get into and maintain flow. Try running with dynamic, rhythmic music while imagining perfect form, using audiogenics.

Summary

Repetition and exaggeration are the tools for reprogramming both mental and physical skills. As such, this rather lengthy summary is designed once again to reprogram your thinking patterns as well as your running. I cannot overemphasize the importance of internalizing the conceptual basis of psychomechanical training.

You learn new patterns of movement by repeating the movements over and over again at the speed and intensity you want to master. What feels exaggerated is usually only a slight change in motor habit. Remember, the primary objective during any kind of speed play is to practice focusing strategies to run faster, longer, and more easily.

By running short segments of touch-and-goes (at a good tempo) followed by complete recoveries (so that you are no longer breathing hard), you accomplish two things:

1. You can concentrate objectively during the running segments.
2. While your muscles are recovering, you can mentally process how the repeat felt and decide what to focus on for the next one.

Like an Indy race car driver, you need to become totally aware of your body's biofeedback (reading the gauges) so that you can adjust your body posture, arm swing, and stride frequency/length as the course changes. As you refine your running biomechanics, you can run faster by effectively focusing plyometric/elastic energy to supplement contractile power in your muscles. When you consider that all muscles and tendons have a degree of elasticity, learning to take advantage of this potential energy makes sense.

The walking drill on page 39 is a great place to start to refine your sensitivity to your biofeedback. Feel your foot contact the ground, nearly flat-footed, under your body, beneath a slightly bent knee. Be aware of how your weight spreads the toes slightly as your body moves over your foot. Focus on swinging the upper arm back and up, cocking the shoulders and thrusting the chest forward as the upper leg extends rearward. Toe off from well behind your body, and feel your body chase your chest as you fall gently forward off your toes. To fine-tune this process, find a place clear of any obstacles, shut your eyes (or better yet, blindfold yourself) and run with your elbow touching a partner's while you "read" your body's "dials and gauges." The beauty of awareness drills is that you can do them almost anywhere and anytime, and you don't have to change clothes or shower afterward.

The next step is to repeat the walking drill while running gently. While you don't want to start out at race pace or effort, you do need to run with a fairly quick turnover rate. The body learns more effectively from repetitions at the goal or faster rate of movement than from practicing the movement at a slower-than-desired rate, so a light, quick turnover is in order. Because everything happens quickly, focus on the sequence of actions required:

1. Preflight—The body needs to be ready to fly. Jog lightly, stretch, pick up the pace a little, and stretch again. Start thinking about how you want to run. Think, "Repeats, good form, light and quick."

2. Rev-up—Before each repeat, run in place at tempo rhythm. Move your awareness into your feet. Feel foot contact, weighting, and toe-off. Sense your heels coming up behind you. Cock your shoulders by swinging your upper arms back and up. Let off the brakes, thrust your chest forward, and start to taxi down the runway.

3. Loading—Feel the muscles in your quads and calves load elastic energy when the knees and ankles bend for an instant as the foot is weighted. Be aware of your upper arms swinging back and up to cock your shoulders as your hip starts to extend rearward and you float over your feet.

4. Firing—Feel your knees straightening and your ankles snapping as your upper arm swings accelerate to the rear, upward position, cocking your shoulders, just as you toe off.

5. Flying—As a natural follow-through to the firing action, focus on thrusting your chest forward, releasing elastic energy from your cocked shoulder to aid the forward arm swing, bending your elbows and knees, and kicking up your heels.

6. Touch-and-goes—In keeping with our flight-training metaphor, focus on each segment, recover, focus on the next, recover, and so on.

Keep your attitude playful and observant during these sessions. Don't time the runs or compare them with past times until the movements feel more natural. If possible, videotape the sessions or run with a partner who can mimic your style. Remember, these sessions are all about learning how efficient running feels. Don't trust how it "feels" to be accurate without some kind of objective visual feedback as validation. If you have trouble getting into the rhythm running on the flat, try light bounding. Here you can magnify your feedback by greatly exaggerating your rearward leg extension/toe-off and upper arm cocking/chest thrust. Slower motion is okay here, because the workload is increased by the longer, exaggerated striding. Go through all the steps described in the preceding list.

Okay, put the book down for a little bit. Time to go solo!

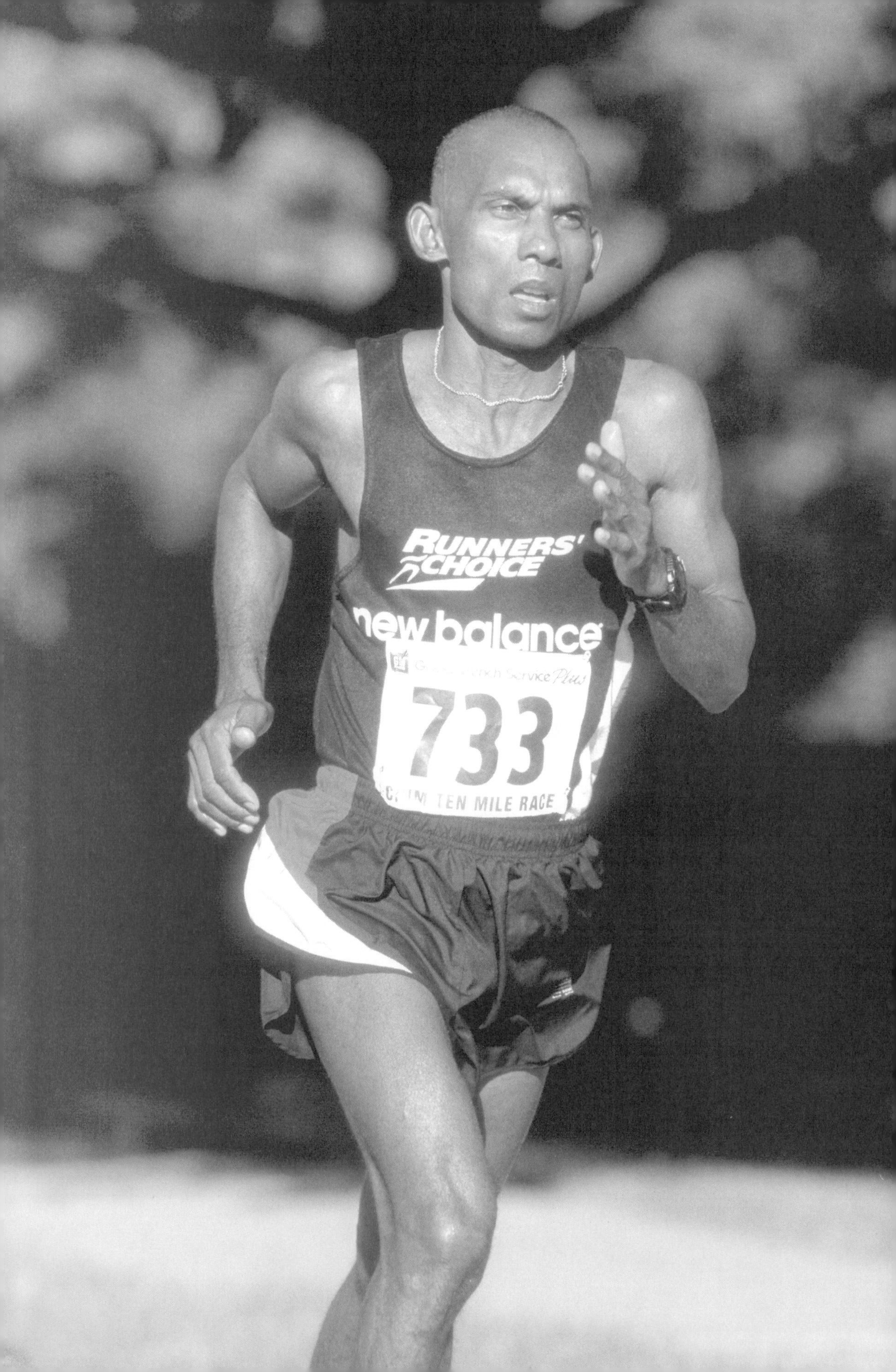
RUNNERS' CHOICE
new balance
733
TEN MILE RACE

4

Mind and Body Control

I first became aware of the impact that my mind has on my physical performance while I was in junior high school. I loved basketball and dreamed of making our school team. I played during every free moment and was deadly from anywhere on the court in my driveway. The same was true of the basket roped to the telephone pole down the street, where the high school kids played every evening and on weekends. Even though I was "a little kid," the big kids let me play with them because of my accuracy, passing ability, and tenacity. During gym class, however, where my goal was to impress Coach Shonesky and be invited to try out for the team, I couldn't even hit the backboard, much less make baskets. My head was full of voices shouting at me, criticizing me, ridiculing me. I became frustrated because I couldn't demonstrate my abilities when it counted. The closest I came to making the team was being student manager.

Years later, in boot camp, I experienced the thrill of coming through under pressure, and I learned a valuable lesson about how my mind works. In the Marine Corps, every Marine is considered a rifleman first, regardless of his military occupational specialty. Therefore, there is considerable pressure to perform well on the rifle range. I had never even held a gun before I enlisted, but the instructors said that was an advantage. Those of us with no prior experience had no bad habits to overcome; we simply had to follow instructions. Because I was already excelling physically and academically, I knew that qualifying as an expert might well lead to promotion from private to private first class when I graduated. I wanted that PFC stripe badly.

On prequalification day, I shot extremely well and, had I "declared" beforehand, I would have shot high expert. I was pumped, and that night I went to bed with visions of my uniform decked out in both my expert's badge and my PFC stripes.

The next morning I was nervous and tense as I assumed the standing position at the 200-yard line. "What's wrong with me?" I asked myself. "Just don't blow this—your future is on the line!" a voice in my head answered. Although I did not shoot badly during slow firing, my performance wasn't nearly as good as on the previous day. Between and sometimes during shots, this critical monologue was going on in my head. Then, we were called for the 200-yard sitting rapid-fire position, and I shot well. Without time to think, I automatically "lined 'em up, held 'em, and squeezed 'em off," as we had been instructed time after time during the two previous weeks.

Feeling a little better, I headed back to the 300-yard line. On the sitting/kneeling slow-fire segment, I experienced a replay not only of the 200-yard slow-fire concentration problems but also of my junior high basketball disappointment. The voice sneered, "Are you going to blow it again?" "No!" I shouted back to myself. Again slow fire was a near disaster. I was so distracted that I almost didn't get off all my rounds within the time limit. Thankfully, the rapid-fire portion went well: I hit all bull's-eyes.

On the way back to the 500-yard line, I hastily calculated that I needed to put nine out of the next 10 shots in the black to shoot expert. By the time I assumed my prone position and started sighting in, I felt nauseous, my hands were sweating, and my eyes were watering. I was going to blow it. Then, in my ear, I heard the voice of senior drill instructor Staff Sergeant Ferrari say quietly, but firmly, "You can do this, Miller. Don't think or keep score. Just hold 'em and squeeze 'em." My first round was just out of the black to the right. Momentarily, I panicked; then I said to myself, "Adjust for the wind, just like in practice." I adjusted my rear sight and the next round was dead center. A calm settled over me as one at a time I "held 'em and squeezed 'em" eight more times—and shot nine bulls in a row. I looked around for SGT Ferrari, but I couldn't find him anywhere on the line. To this day, I don't know if he really encouraged me or if my mind imagined him there for support. This little anecdote has repeated itself in various forms throughout my life and the lives of the many athletes with whom I have had the privilege to work. Although the inner voice is often negative, sometimes it coaches us instead. There's a lesson here: *the conscious mind can only focus effectively on one thing at a time, and you can choose what that thing is.*

Emotional flooding, a response to what you have chosen to think about, disrupts your ability to perform. In other words, *attentional control* (control of what, when, and how you think) is the key to managing your emotions to keep them from disrupting your performance. To develop attentional control and emotion management skills, you must understand that your mind controls your body in much the same manner as a pilot's control and guidance systems control the flight characteristics of a plane.

Your Control Center

So where do these "voices" come from? Exactly who is doing the talking and who is doing the listening? Who's in charge, anyway? These questions are important. To answer them, let's take a look at what I've learned about how our minds work from science and from my experience with athletes and other performers at all levels.

The Dual Computer

Obviously, what goes on in your head before and while you run influences how you are running at any given moment. Your brain can be described as the control center of your running machine. In this control center is the most complex computer on earth, but, unfortunately, it comes with no operator's manual. Not only does the brain lack instructions, but it is also programmed slightly differently in each of us, depending upon our genetic gifts and environmental influences. Great performers have figured out how to use their control-center capabilities to enhance their performances. Less consistent performers often let their control centers run free, interfering with their concentration and distracting them from the task at hand. Fortunately, our brains share enough common components that we can build a credible model of the brain as a dual computer, each half having its own program technician and requisite capabilities and responsibilities.

Remember the "mental team" concept that I developed after running so well in Boston? Well, science again provides support for that intuitive paradigm. Hemispheric brain research shows that the right and left hemispheres do perform both similar and different functions. The brain itself can be thought of as a dual, bilateral computer whose halves share memory but have different programming capabilities.

In developing this model, I have drawn heavily on the research and development associated with studies into the hemispheric functions of the brain. Each of our two brain hemispheres, the right and left, seems to be typically associated with characteristic functions. How each half works independently and cooperatively is the subject of continuing, fascinating, and often conflicting research. While my model borrows heavily from the hemispheric function research, studies, and application, it is not meant to parallel bilateral brain function in every respect. My dual-computer model is designed to provide you with a mechanism by which you can better manage your thoughts and emotions and control your physical responses during competition.

Right Brain Versus Left Brain

The right brain functions like an analog computer, while the left is more like a digital computer. Most everyone is familiar with digital computers. They follow exact sequences of steps, address one item at a time, and produce one solution for each problem. Similarly, the left brain deals primarily with verbal tasks, analysis, organization, planning, judgment, evaluation, and *ego-speak* (rational thought). Analog computers, on the other

Learning to manage your thoughts and responses during training will help improve your performance during competition.

hand, produce an array of solutions to any one problem and are able to address several issues at one time. The right brain is best suited to run performance programs. Athletic, musical, and artistic skills, along with intuition, creativity, and imagination, are generally attributed to the right brain.

Fine-motor skills are programmed into your right brain through repetition, but when your left brain senses fatigue, loss of form, or changes in terrain, wind, or weather, it can enhance or maintain those skills by responding with appropriate image-enhancing words (audiogenic programs). Alternatively, your left brain (the voice) can disrupt or inhibit the run functions programmed by your right brain. What comes to mind with the following words, and what do you think the performance outcomes will be? "I don't want to strike out," (or "hit it in the water," "look stupid," etc.). "I love this course and always run well here."

You can program your right brain to alert your left brain to sensory feedback, such as muscle tightness, stitches, labored breathing, uphills/downhills, changes in energy expenditure rates, and inefficient muscular movement. Your left brain can then use image-enhancing words to direct your right brain to make appropriate adjustments to your running technique. Over time, your right brain will learn to respond automatically to sensory input by adjusting stride length, stride frequency, hand position, arm swing, posture, and breathing with minimal involvement from your left brain. During hard training and racing, you have to program your dual computers so that they don't interfere with each other's functions. How you think during the last sets of hard intervals or at the end of long runs will be reflected in your racing. You will do exactly what you have been practicing in training. Change your thinking to improve your running.

Reprogramming Your Mind

In an earlier section, I bad-mouthed interval training as being the sole means of becoming faster, because chasing times around a track will not automatically result in increased leg speed and strength. Intelligent use of track time, however, can help you tune in to what it feels like to run faster with perfect form. Advocates of track work have done intervals for years and have learned the feel of running fast (right-brain function). Most novice runners become wrapped up in their interval times (left-brain function). The clock is only one means of feedback, and chasing times keeps you in left-brain mode, where you focus on the effort, inhibiting fluid, right-brain movement. More important feedback is your sense of strength, fluid movement, coordinated arm/leg swings, soft foot plants, and harmony among your breathing, rhythmic movement, and effort. Again, consider the race car driver. If the only factors he considered were his place and speed, and he ignored coolant temperature, oil pressure, and fuel consumption, how well would you expect him to do in a long race? You have to learn to read the subtle sensory information during your training so that, during the big races, your left brain will remain quiet and allow your right brain to execute its performing programs. Audiogenics, thought-stopping, counting, visualization, imagery, and other strategies form the basis for your reprogramming.

Through repetition, simulation training, and mental rehearsal, you can also program your right brain to alert you to changes in mental, emotional, social, and environmental demands by signaling your left brain of changes in your physical responses to these elements. Once alerted, your left brain can activate the appropriate program to deal with these issues immediately, reducing anxiety and worry, preventing loss of concentration, and maintaining skilled motor movements. You need to develop several alternative strategies to develop, refine, maintain, and, when necessary, reactivate effective programs that lead to peak performances.

Peak Performances

Most of us have experienced peak performances. Remember those early fall mornings when the air was crisp, your steps light, and the running incredibly easy? Is this common experience different than those of the world-record-winning performers?

Over the years, sport psychologists have investigated this phenomenon. They report that during or after peak performances, athletes typically

- have positive task confidence in their capabilities and preparation;

- have high self-concepts (they feel good about themselves as people);
- feel totally absorbed in the performance and detached from everything else;
- do not have the common feelings of pain, effort, and fatigue;
- experience time distortion, feeling as though they are totally locked into each moment within the performance;
- perform automatically, with little or no conscious effort;
- expect to succeed;
- act completely in the moment;
- are totally focused on what they are doing;
- experience a sense of power and of being completely immersed in the activity; and
- have trouble recalling all or parts of the performance.

Many modern sport psychologists promote these peak performances, also known as being *in the zone,* as the goal for every athlete. While I have on occasion found myself in a similar state, I cannot remember ever making it happen, nor have I ever found an athlete who knew how to flip the in-the-zone switch whenever he or she wanted to. I am presenting my ideas, paradigms, and suggestions in the hope that, by adopting and adapting some of the concepts, you will be able to train and race more consistently and develop a higher sense of control before and during your performances. The secret to achieving this goal consistently is learning to manage how, when, and what you think before and during races. Sounds easy—so what's the problem? Why do even elites sometimes choke? My answer is that they, and possibly you, may sometimes have undisciplined program technicians.

Program Technicians

Our society in general and school systems in particular are very often error-correction-based learning institutions. Many parents are much more prone to correct and admonish children to modify their behavior than to reinforce more positive actions. *Should*s are programmed into our left brains at an early age, and for many of us they become our dominant way of thinking. Imagine a pushy, self-centered, loudmouthed pip-squeak of a program technician in charge of running your left brain. On the other hand, imagine your right-brain program technician as a quiet, shy, exceptionally skilled individual who requires a quiet, calm environment in which to work. I think you can see the problem. If not directed to run positive programs, our left-brain techs will look for something wrong and run their *critic* programs. How many times have you gotten early, unexpectedly fast splits and said to yourself, "Oh, no. Too fast. Better slow down," instead of "How's my breathing? How do my legs feel? Maybe it's short or downhill"? Whether you get a split that is too fast or too slow, you need your left-brain tech to run a sensory-feedback program and then make a technique/effort decision.

Programming Tactics

You can use several tactics to keep your left-brain tech in line so that your right-brain tech can engage the appropriate skills programs. Thought-stopping is usually the first step. Just order your left-brain tech, "Shut up." Then direct a more positive program to be run.

For example, I had been training ultrarunner Laurie Staton one winter. Because we ran together on several of her longer, harder training runs, she suggested that I run the Nugget 50-miler later in the spring. I remember lining up for the predawn start and hearing the race director announce, "Welcome to the Nugget 50, one of the toughest races in America." "What are you doing here? You're no ultrarunner," my left-brain tech immediately chimed in. "Shut up. For the rest of this race, I don't want to hear anything from you unless it's positive," I said to myself. Until mile 43, everything went great. Then I said to myself, "Now it's time for the hard miles." The next mile was the longest of the race, but by the end of it the sports drink kicked in, my blood sugar stabilized, and I said to my left-brain tech, "Nice try, but I'm on to you. Get back to work." I finished in a decent time and was pleased with my overall performance.

Audiogenics is another effective method to engage your left-brain tech in more productive work. Repeating image-enhancing and form-reinforcing words does two things. First, because your left brain can only perform one verbal task at a time, the repetition stops your left-brain tech from harassing you and distracting your focus from the task at hand. Second, it allows your right-brain tech to execute the right brain's responsibilities, uninhibited. During the last part of short, intense races or the closing miles of a marathon, patterned counting of your exhales in rhythm with your footsteps accomplishes the same thing as more complex choices of audiogenic words. At the end of a marathon, I often can't think much past "One, two, three, one, two, three. . . ." At these moments, my focus is to maintain stride length and frequency by concentrating on compact arm swing and balanced forward posture.

Requiring your left brain and right brain to work together is essential in your overall performance programming because of the nature of distance running. Unlike gymnastics, skiing, and other nonendurance sports, which only take minutes or less to complete, distance running and other endurance events can take hours. It is impossible to run trance-like throughout a marathon. During these long runs, your program techs have ample opportunity to get on each other's nerves and disrupt your performance. Thought-stopping, audiogenics, and counting are tactics that you can use to direct or redirect your attention, activate or reactivate appropriate performance programming, and manage your emotions. Otherwise you may often find yourself subject to not just an occasional interfering thought but raging debates about the value of what you are doing, who you are, and why you keep doing this to yourself.

Why do the best-made racing plans so often go down the tubes accompanied by internal ranting and raving? The answer, obviously, is that there must be some computer virus that disrupts the racing programs we have so carefully prepared to execute. Our toughest competition is not the course or the other runners but "the little voice inside me telling me to stop." (Zachariassen 1990) Where does this voice come from, and what can you do about it?

© Victah Sailer

Thought-stopping, audiogenics, and counting are all tactics to help keep out the interfering thoughts that can have such a negative impact on performance.

Critic and Emotion Management

> The *pathological critic* is a term coined by psychologist Eugene Sagan to describe the negative inner voice that attacks and judges you. . . . The critic *blames* you for things that go wrong. The critic *compares* you to others. . . . The critic *sets impossible standards* of perfection and then beats you up for the smallest mistake. The critic keeps an album of your past failures, but never once reminds you of your strengths or accomplishments. The critic has a script describing how you *ought* to live and screams that you are wrong or bad if your needs drive you to violate his rules. The critic tells you to be the best—and if you're not the best, you are nothing. He *calls you names*. . . and makes you believe that all of them are true, The critic reads your friends' minds and convinces you that they are bored, turned off, disappointed, or disgusted by you. The critic *exaggerates* your weaknesses by insisting that you *always* say stupid things, *always* screw up relationships, or *never* finish anything on time. (italics added) (McKay and Fanning 1987, 15)

The first time I read those words, I could not believe how accurately they described what went on in my head during disappointing performance situations, such as blowing a test I had prepared for, taking my driver's test the first time, or trying to get up the nerve to ask for a date. Later, when running became important to me, I sometimes experienced the same thing. The italicized words emphasize cues that can alert you to the fact that your personal critic program is running and will inhibit the execution of your performer programs. This book, *Self Esteem*, turned out to be a treasure of information about the voice and how to manage it. Reading it set off a number of *aha*s in my head. When the voice directs personal criticisms toward you (calling you names, putting you down, comparing you to others, etc.— making judgments about you as a person based on how you are running), that's a sure sign that the *ego* virus is interfering with your performing program. Your left-brain technician has programmed your self-worth to be based on how you run.

McKay and Fanning also discuss the uniquely human concept of self-esteem and the major problem associated with that concept. As humans, we have the capacity to define our own identity. There are no universal norms as to what that identity should represent, however, so we develop our own values to measure our performance.

When faster times become the sole measure of your self-worth, you set yourself up for failure and disappointment. How you run does not define who you are.

As I read this, more lights started coming on. We all have the capability to define for ourselves what kind of people we want to be. Athletes tend to define themselves based upon their athletic results. They are only as good or bad as their last performance. That's a tremendous psychological load to carry during a competition. If you race well, you are a good person. If you race poorly, you are a bad person. If you run fast in one race, you have to run even better in the next. To become a better runner, you also have to become a better person. You have to change who you are, and you can't do that. When faster times become the sole measure of your self-worth and self-esteem, you are setting yourself up for failure and disappointment—unfairly!

In other words, the need to feel special is within each of us. Everyone wants to feel important and appreciated. But society does a poor job of defining exactly what an individual must do to reach those goals.

As runners, we tend to define who we are by how we run. As humans, we need to feel special and unique. As human runners, we tie these two concepts together. Add in the prestige and admiration heaped on athletic heroes, and we find ourselves trapped. I believe that the great popularity of marathons is related to the fact that just finishing one defines you as a *marathoner*—a special kind of runner—regardless of how long it took.

Enter the critic, the left-brain program that runs constantly. It has developed since birth to ensure that you do what you *should, ought to,* and *must* do to gain recognition and acceptance from those you deem important. In a society where most of us start our learning by hearing "No, no, Tommy," and proceed through an educational system that is based almost entirely on error correction, our left brains become overprogrammed, overused, and overbearing.

So how do elite athletes overcome interference by their left-brain programming during competition? Several factors come into play. First is the nature of the athletes' sports. The challenge is very different in activities that take seconds to complete compared to those that take much longer. Another factor is the speed and continuity of the action. Whether the sport is a team or individual activity also influences concentration.

Elite athletes seem to separate who they are as people from what they are doing during the competition. This is not to say that they are not ego-driven. Ego is what compels them to train, sacrifice, and prepare to compete. Before they head for the starting line, however, they leave their egos and their left-brain programs with their warm-ups and surrender to the task at hand. They have found ways to expand the capabilities of their right brains so that their left brains interfere minimally during contests.

Let's now turn to ways that you can first deprogram the critic's influence and then reprogram your left brain's capabilities to assist you in your running and racing.

Letting the Coach and Critic Work Together

McKay and Fanning point out that two kinds of self-esteem problems are associated with your internal critic—situational and characterological. *Situational self-esteem* relates to specific areas, such as public speaking, dating, or performing. A person might be self-conscious about speaking in public but self-confident in other areas, such as sports, math, art, or music. Situational self-esteem problems can be effectively handled by developing new skills and strategies. *Characterological self-esteem* problems, on the other hand, are more global and are rooted in a person's sense (or lack) of identity. While people who suffer from characterological self-esteem problems can benefit from developing new skills and strategies to cope with specific issues, professional counseling may be required to transform the negative self-image into a more positive one. Indicators include extreme sensitivity to criticism and a constant tendency to put yourself down. These more serious problems are well beyond the scope of this book, which deals with understanding, identifying, developing, and refining situational performing skills that you can apply in your running, racing, educational, and professional interactions.

An old saying asserts, "We set goals according to our dreams, but perform according to our fears." This truism is the work of our critics. Prerace anxiety and worry often develop as soon as you decide to run an important race. For weeks or months you worry about all the things that could go wrong and lead to your failure. How much anxiety and worry you experience usually relates directly to how much you base your self-worth on the results. You don't have to run races. You race for psychological reasons, and you connect the results to your identity. Logically, you know that your order of finish or time does not define you as a person, but you feel as though it does. Your greatest fear, and the source of your anxiety, is that you won't live up to your own expectations, much less anyone else's. Instead of focusing on better ways to prepare, your mind is preoccupied with everything that can go wrong. Sometimes you dread trying to reach your goal. Your critic is hard at work.

The critic program runs exclusively on the left-brain component of your dual brain. This program utilizes the analytical, logical, verbal, and digital capabilities of your mind. As long as you let the critic dominate your left brain with worry and anxiety, you seriously inhibit your ability to set goals, assess performance demands, develop training strategies, and apply racing tactics. You are the owner of your sport franchise (body and mind), and you must assert your authority. There is room for both your inner critic and an inner coach. Only one, however, can use your left brain at a time. Let your *coach* program technician help you prepare for and execute your training and racing strategies. Allow your *critic* program technician to analyze and evaluate your training and performance, but on a noninterference basis. The best way to do this is through comprehensive performance planning, which covers the seven demand areas—functional, physical, mental/emotional, social, logistical, environmental, and technical—and requires extensive involvement of both left-brain program technicians. The coach is responsible for coming up with ways to train and prepare, while the critic develops methods to evaluate and test progress. (Chapter 6 covers performance programming in more detail).

Your prerace anxiety will diminish when your inner coach and critic work together to do the following:

- Set realistic racing goals over which you have a measure of control (In other words, decide how you are going to race to achieve your goal. *Remember that prerace anxiety is often your body's signal to you that your ego has set a goal your body is not prepared to reach. You must develop and adjust your goals according to your training achievements.)*
- Assess all race demands and develop strategies to meet them
- Set measurable objectives in each demand area to evaluate training progress
- Develop prerace planning and race programming based on training results
- Evaluate race results not just on time and place but also— more importantly—on the effectiveness of your planning, training, and race program execution

On-Course "Voice" Management

During the course of a race or hard training run, I find that my inner critic is more of a nagger than a yeller or screamer. I call him Howard after the old sports announcer Howard Cosell, who was on Monday Night Football when I was getting hooked on racing. Howard the Nagger would take a split time at mile one or two and then project my finish time. If it wasn't what he expected, he would nag me about it, quietly at first, by saying things like "Too slow, better hurry—won't set a PR at this pace." I would count or do audiogenics for a while, and then he'd break back into my consciousness. If I was off target pace toward the end, Howard often piped up, "See I told you. Don't blame me; you're the one who's not running fast enough." If I happened to pull off an exceptional race—usually because I'd managed to keep Howard quiet and my inner coach, Vince (after legendary coach Vince Lombardi of the Green Bay Packers), in line throughout the race—Howard would wait until after the finish. Vince and I would be discussing in my head how easy and focused the race had been. Inevitably, Howard would butt in: "If it was so easy, think how much better it would have been if you had really tried." Finally I realized that Howard worked for me, not the other way around. I redefined his job description and required that he and Vince work together cooperatively.

You know your critic program is running when the "voice" attacks you with personal remarks: blaming, comparing, name calling, failure history recall, exaggerations, and failure projections. Here are some final tips from McKay and Fanning on how to manage your critic and emotions:

- *Personalize your critic.* Giving it a name and identity gives you someone you can deal with.

- *Stop your thoughts.* You can override the critic's verbal program when you tell the voice, "Shut up" or, "I'll deal with you later," count exhales, repeat audiogenic mantras, or recite "Poetry in Motion" (see page 56).

- *Challenge the critic.* By answering the critic's attack with, "Says who?" you identify the source. Remind the critic that there will be an opportunity to offer judgments *after* the race is over, not during it.

- *Postpone judgment.* Focus on objective performing cues during competition, and wait until after the race to analyze and evaluate your overall performance.

Focus on the task at hand and wait until after the race to evaluate your overall performance.

Summary

Your brain can be viewed as a dual computer, made up of a left brain and a right brain, each with its own capabilities. While the right brain is best suited for specific, highly skilled, refined motor tasks, the left brain is more of a general purpose component. The functional characteristics of left-brain programming include logic, analytical thinking, tactical planning, strategies, criticism, detail specificity, verbal instructions, voluntary control, serial (sequential) processing, determination, trying, and effort (Unestahl 1983). Notice that patterned, skilled, fine-motor movement is *not* included on the list of left-brain functions. Your left brain has only a rudimentary motor movement program.

Your running performances depend on how well you can foresee changing demands and build in appropriate responses. Your right brain is capable of coming up with many solutions for each problem. You then need to reengage your left brain to choose the appropriate solution for each specific problem.

A variety of metaphors reinforce the different ways in which you can learn to manage your right- and left-brain capabilities more effectively. Personalize your right- and left-brain program technicians and remind them that they have to work together, under your direction, as a performance team. Assign each technician appropriate tasks, and hold the technicians responsible for their execution. Separate who you are from what you do. Remember that running and racing are things you do, not who you are. A disappointing performance doesn't mean something is wrong with you. Rather, it is a reflection of your preparation and execution strategies—things you can change and refine. In fact, those strategies are the subject of the remaining chapters.

5

Competitive Mindset

Many conflicting and supporting forces influence your ability to perform at your best during the big race or any other important performing situation. This chapter examines the array of forces that act on your mind before and during events, so that you can manage them effectively and reach your performance potential.

The performance blueprint depicted in figure 5.1 is based on my own years of competing and coaching, observations gleaned from years of working with elite performers from a number of sports, and the basic concepts of performance psychology. The blueprint links together many of the concepts discussed in earlier chapters. It establishes the relationships they have with each other in a *mind map*—a schematic of the various forces that affect your ability to perform. The blueprint uses a graphic representation to reinforce these concepts in a compact, easily understood, logical manner.

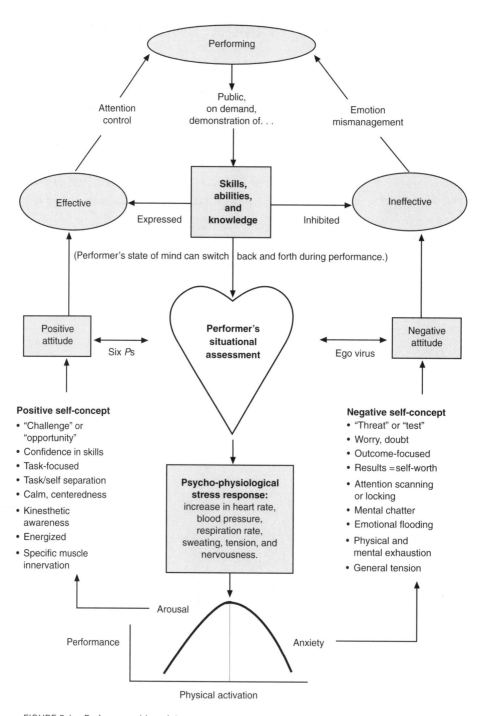

FIGURE 5.1 Performance blueprint.

Effective Versus Ineffective Performances

Start at the top of the blueprint with *performing*. Following the downward arrow is a working definition: *Public, on demand, demonstration of skills, abilities, and knowledge.* Remember my frustration when I couldn't impress my basketball coach? I had the capabilities, but when he was watching (*public demonstration*), something happened that *inhibited* (right arrow) my performance, resulting in an *ineffective* performance. I couldn't handle my emotions (*mismanagement*) because I was focused on the wrong things.

On the other hand, my breakthrough on the 500-yard line of the rifle range allowed me to *express* (left arrow) my shooting skills under pressure. The real or imagined advice received from my senior drill instructor inspired me to focus my attention *effectively* (*attention control*).

Now that we understand effective and ineffective performing, let's unlock the puzzle of why each happens.

Situational Assessment

At the heart of your ability to perform when, where, and how you want is your *situational assessment*, depicted in the heart on the diagram. The nature of your assessment determines whether your performance will be effective or not. Notice also that this assessment is not fixed. It can shift back and forth during the competition. Think of Lasse Viren in the 1972 Olympic 10K. Early in the race, he got knocked to the ground. By the time he regrouped and took off again, the pack was nearly half a lap in front of him. His initial reaction was probably unprintable. Fueled with a new surge of adrenaline, however, he stormed back to win the gold medal. By reassessing his situation, he converted a potential disappointment into success. Let's continue down the diagram before returning to *attitude*.

One of the feelings typical to athletes in performance situations is the *psycho-physiological stress response:* your heart rate, blood pressure, respiration rate, sweating, tension, and nervousness automatically increase as a result of how you assess your situation. In the case of effective performing, you experience a sense of *arousal*—a readiness to perform. Your degree of *physical activation* is appropriate for the task at hand. In an ineffective performance, however, you are overwhelmed by *anxiety*—worry and doubt about the results of what you are about to attempt. Arousal readies you, while anxiety distracts you. Whether you are aroused or anxious depends on your situational assessment and the state of mind and *attitude* it inspires.

Attitude

Many sports writers and coaches talk about attitude making the difference, but rarely have I heard them define the components of positive or negative attitudes in terms that are useful and applicable. So let's discuss attitude. Notice the two horizontal arrows extending from the heart of the diagram. The *six* Ps—Proper Prior Programming Promotes "Phocused" Performing—lead to a *positive attitude,* a way of thinking that enhances performance. (The six *P*s are discussed in more detail in chapter 6.) On the other hand, the *ego virus* produces a *negative attitude,* a way of thinking that inhibits performance.

Remember my experience at the World Blind Marathon Championship? As long as Harry and I were wrapped up in the ego-related ramifications of failing, the potential for success was poor. Once we reassessed our situation and refocused on what we knew we could do, the potential for success was greater, and it was redefined in terms that didn't center only on winning. By changing our assessment from, "We have to win," (over which we had limited control) to, "If we run our most skillful race, we can live with the results," we neutralized our ego viruses and reduced our levels of anxiety. As we refocused our mental energies on developing a plan to run our most skillful race, our physical activation state shifted to arousal—the state of readiness.

Let's take a closer look at the contrasting elements that are common to effective and ineffective performances, according to the cockpit recordings of elite athletes and psychologists.

When it comes to effective performances, attitude makes all the difference.

Self-Concept

In effective performances, athletes typically feel good about themselves as people. They may not feel that way in less successful ventures. The difference is often whether they assess the situation as a *challenge*—an *opportunity* to demonstrate their skills, abilities, and knowledge—or as a *threat*, or *test,* to their self-image or ego. Those who come into the contest with a high degree of *confidence* in their skills and preparation are much more likely to succeed than those who are full of *worry* and *doubt.*

A positive attitude is *task-focused*, while a negative attitude focuses on outcomes. The task-oriented focus allows athletes to separate who they are from what they are doing. *Outcome-focused* athletes, on the other hand, are constantly judging their progress toward the final result (and, consciously or subconsciously, their self-worth), which inhibits the running of their performing programs.

In an ineffective performance, the left-brain technician, which has a limited motor program but a dominating ego program, selfishly takes over the operation. Athletes typically say that during ineffective performances their minds are either freewheeling, bouncing from one thing to another, or locked into a single focus: *attentional scanning or locking.* Constant negative, critical *mental chatter* gives rise to *emotional flooding*, which continues to short-circuit the brain of the ineffective performer.

Effective performers, in contrast, often report a sense of *calm* and *centeredness* as they hone in on the task at hand. They let go of everything else at that moment. They don't push other thoughts out of their minds, as is so often reported. Sports reporters, athletes, and coaches often describe mental toughness as the ability to force everything out of the mind except task focus. In reality, that perspective results in tension, not intensity. Consistently successful athletes have repeatedly expressed to me the importance of "letting go" of interrupting thoughts rather than "keeping them out."

During peak performances, like Alan Webb's sub-four-minute mile, runners typically report feeling totally absorbed in the performance, letting go of all interrupting thoughts.

When performing effectively, athletes report a heightened sense of body awareness *(kinesthetic awareness)* and are *energized* as their minds prepare to execute the performing programs. They maintain these sensory cues during the activity, especially when they are executing in accordance with their mental rehearsals. Rather than feeling *tense* and *physically and mentally drained* as a result of their worry, doubt, and anxiety, effective performers are ready! *Specific muscle innervation* directed by their right-brain performing programs are fired up and ready to go.

The performance blueprint has proven to be a valuable tool both for analyzing individual performances and for identifying consistent problem areas with athletes' control-center operations and flight guidance systems. Not everyone responds well to this kind of pictorial summary, however, so here is another approach to bring together these concepts and relationships. I'm restating the same type of information in a slightly different form to continue to reprogram your old paradigms—these perceptions won't go away easily.

A Running Philosophy

Let's review what you've learned concerning competition/prerace anxiety, self-concept, and performance. First, you're better able to perform up to your capabilities when you feel good about yourself and are confident that you have the skills and preparation necessary to meet the performance demands. You don't need to be fully aware of either or both conditions, however, for them to be influential. The presence or absence of one or the other can provide the emotional fuel to generate an effective performance (arousal) or to drain you of your emotional energy, leaving you feeling flat. Think of how well you ran after getting that big promotion, date, or other form of recognition—even though those events had nothing to do with your running. Remember how hard it was to run when everything seemed to be going wrong in the rest of your life? On the other hand, athletes often surprise themselves in races of little importance, where they are totally involved in expressing their capabilities.

Your Runs Don't Define You

The ability to define an identity is a uniquely human characteristic, and developing measures of that identity provides meaning in our lives. Measuring our self-worth seems to be inherent in how we view ourselves and how we (our egos) want others to view us. This constant tendency to judge and evaluate ourselves produces many of our personal problems, including, in my opinion, performance anxiety. Because there are no universal norms by which to judge self-worth, we each develop our own standards or borrow them from others. Our basic values are typically instilled in us at an early age by our parents, family, teachers, and religious leaders. About the time we take up sports, we also assume the values of our peer groups. All these values help define behaviors that are "good" and "bad" and that reflect the general norms of our society. We learn how to act to get along with others—but that is not enough. We still have the basic needs for recognition, acceptance, and love that are related to our desire to feel important, special, and appreciated as unique individuals. Each of us wants to stand apart from the crowd in some way, and we seek ways to meet this need.

One of the ways people seek to establish an identity is to become identified as part of a special group (gang, church, team, club, etc.) and to develop unique or high levels of skills within that community. A person who joins a group accepts the group's norms and works to live up to them. While many of us began running to lose weight, get more fit, or reduce stress, we continue for other reasons once those goals have been met. We start to race and want to be called not "joggers" but "runners." We learn that times and distances reflect status in the running community. Therefore, we take up the challenge of improving our racing. We read running magazines and books, experiment with speed work and longer runs, seek coaching advice, and invest in the latest in shoes and running gear. As our times get faster, we feel better about ourselves because we have measurable evidence that we are getting better.

Working toward and achieving racing goals gives meaning to our training and lives. To some extent, we have now defined who we are (runners) and how to measure how good we are (through our times and places). We feel great when we achieve PRs or finally beat competitors who usually finish in front of us, and we're disappointed in ourselves when we don't. This is especially true for runners who come to the sport as adults, those who are getting back into running, and those who don't see themselves as special in other aspects of their lives and are seeking meaning in their lives through their running.

While achieving racing goals helps give meaning to your training and life, how fast you run should never be the sole measure of your self-worth.

For a while there is steady improvement. Sooner or later, however, we reach the inevitable performance plateau. Our times no longer improve, and we start to question, "What's wrong with me?" We train harder, longer, and more often, but still we make little or no improvement. Races that used to be fun, exciting, and challenging are now sources of anxiety, frustration, and disappointment. While we spend our training dreaming of a breakthrough, the reality of a race is like a slap in the face. We become obsessed with improving our times. Those of us who recognized early in our careers that we don't possess natural speed turn to marathons, where just finishing establishes us as "runners"—at least in the community at large.

What's wrong with this approach, and what can *you* do about it? Philosophically, the problem lies in how you are defining and measuring yourself. You are caught in the time/place trap. It doesn't matter whether you are an Olympian, a high schooler, or an age grouper—you can fall into the trap even if the only one you have to answer to is your own ego. You have been programmed as a runner to evaluate your races by this single parameter. The advantage to this simplistic approach is that it is very easy to measure. The disadvantage is that it leads to a very shortsighted view of racing. You are only as good or bad as your last race. This concept is ludicrous. It reflects shallow thinking. Interestingly, this line of thinking is often found in gifted athletes who have been tightly focused on developing their athletic ability since an early age, at the expense of the rest of their development—it is the only way they have to define themselves.

How fast you run does *not* reflect what kind of person you are any more than does the number of degrees, awards, possessions, or achievements you have. By so narrowly defining yourself as a person, you limit your ability to learn, develop, and grow as a human through *doing* the activities of running and racing. Sure, most world-class athletes embrace the tunnel-visioned approach and have achieved extraordinary athletic success. But at what price? What kind of people are they? Many are self-centered, egotistical jerks who happen to have been blessed with great natural talent. Many of these gifted athletes even bemoan the fact that the public doesn't appreciate them as people. I once had an interesting conversation with a multiple Olympic medallist and former world record holder. When I asked if the isolation and sacrifice had been worthwhile, he responded, "What are all the medals and records worth if you have no one to share them with?"

As I see it, how fast you run is primarily a reflection of your physical capabilities, the vast majority of which are genetically determined and only marginally influenced through training. I agree with D.W. Johnson's assertion: "Our identity is built out of our relationships with other people. . . . From the reflections of others, we develop a clear and accurate picture of ourselves. . . . It is within our relationships that we discover who we are as [people]" (1981, 2–3).

Focus on developing and refining strategies to handle the demands of racing, and the results will take care of themselves.

Focus on the Process and the Results Will Come

While you can't change your genetic makeup, you can learn to handle yourself better in the racing/performing situation. Remember how, in the introduction to this book, I shared that my racing and running improved once I started focusing on *how* I was running? The same is true of the psychological part of performing. Focus on understanding, developing, and refining strategies to handle the demands of racing (performing), and the results will take care of themselves.

When you look at racing as a process rather than a result, you have an opportunity to grow and develop as a person. Racing is a performing art based on scientific training. Think about it! Not only are you the artist, but you're also the audience (who else knows exactly what's going on inside you?) and patron (one who gives the artist the opportunity to perform). Measuring your performance exclusively by your time or place is like judging a concert or ballet only on how the last measure of music or dance was performed.

Set Performance Goals

Great performances are the product of extensive planning, preparation, training, and practicing to develop the requisite skills, abilities, and knowledge. When you develop performance measures to evaluate all these aspects, you gain not only a more realistic basis to judge your overall performance but also valuable information on which you can build the next performance.

You begin the process by setting performance goals. Having a goal motivates you to train to accomplish the goal, giving meaning and direction to your actions. Goals serve as a reference to determine performance demands, assess your current capabilities, and develop the training objectives, methods, and measurements that will raise your current capabilities to the level that the goal demands.

After you set goals, the next step is to anticipate the performance demands of your goal, objectively assess your current capabilities, and contrast the two. For example, if you have good 5K and 10K speed but die in longer races, you have to improve your endurance. If you can run forever but lack speed, you need to work on strength, power, and leg speed. To remedy weaknesses and exploit strengths, you must develop progressive, measurable training objectives. Finally, as the big race nears, do a time trial as a reality check to help you decide whether to keep or modify your original goal based on your actual training achievements. Remember to base your goals on factors that you control.

Prepare for Anything

From the perspective of physical training, these recommendations all are common sense. Nonetheless, the physical demands alone are rarely the source of athletes' worry, doubt, and anxiety. The key to recognizing the source of these emotions lies in the control factor. Because runners attend almost exclusively to the physical preparation for racing, they often ignore the mental, emotional, social, logistical, environmental, and technical demands that are inherent in each race. When you fail to prepare to meet one or more of these demands and something happens that you don't expect, such as rain, wind, or extreme temperatures, you panic and feel out of control. You can't sleep. Others get on your nerves easily. You feel emotionally and physically drained. Your mind won't rest but fills your head with chatter about what you should've done and how you will fail—and I'd bet with the mind on that one, unless you take back control.

Racing is not primarily an intellectual or mental activity—but comprehensive training and preparation is. Racing is a physical act—the more physical the better! Use your left brain to plan for, rehearse, experiment with, and evaluate all aspects of the upcoming race. Arrive at the starting line with a clear strategy of exactly what physical and mental skills you are going to focus on from warm-up through each section of the course. Turn on your right brain during mental rehearsal and warm-up. Get your engine up to speed, and execute your racing program to the best of your abilities. If you have done all the proper programming, you can do it! If something unexpected does come up, make a decision or adjustment and continue running each mile as efficiently and skillfully as you can.

Evaluate Your Performance

After the race is over, evaluate your performance based on how well you managed all aspects of the race, from the moment you decided to run it through the preparation, training, and, finally, the actual execution of your race plan. Often this approach leads to new PRs. More often it doesn't. It is all right to be disappointed in your time or place, but a poor time doesn't mean "You suck!"

It means that you need to refine your race programming skills—
and that's all it means!

Summary

The true measure of yourself, as reflected in your racing, is not
your finishing time or place but your ability to establish challenging performance goals over which you can exercise direct
control; to develop and test a progressive training program to
meet the performance demands; to manage and control your
emotions and attention before and during the competition; and
to race skillfully and efficiently from start to finish. The *process*
is what makes you a winner.

It is this process-oriented approach to performing that allows
elite athletes to perform so well, so consistently. By letting go of
self and maintaining effective *task focus,* they are able to handle
the demands of racing—and the results simply take care of themselves.

6

Performance Programming

Refining your biomechanics and psychomechanics does no good if you show up at the wrong time, have the wrong shoes or gear, or don't know about the long uphill finish. The secret to performing consistently and the key to unlocking your performance potential is preparing to meet the functional (course-specific), physical, mental, emotional, social, logistical, technical, and environmental demands for each race. In this chapter, you learn to put it all together. This chapter takes you from the decision to enter the big race through the preparation process, performance planning, program execution, and postevent assessment.

The following story, which describes the preparation and execution strategies that then-66-year-old John Cahill developed for his first marathon, helps illustrate many of the concepts in this chapter. After only a year of running, John ran a 3:04 in his first marathon. At age 73, he followed a similar approach and ran a 3:05.

Planning to Meet Your Goals

Ring, ring, ring. *"Hello, this is Tom."* "Did you write the *Utah Sports Guide* article on the St. George Marathon?" *"Yes."* "Good. My name is John Cahill and I want an appointment tomorrow morning. What time can I see you?" *"9:30, and it won't be free."* "Fine, I'll see you then." My first impression of John was not very positive.

The next morning, a red Porsche convertible hesitated briefly as it went by the "tenant parking only" sign and braked to a stop in front of my apartment. Out stepped what appeared to be a skinny, geriatric hippie with shoulder-length, lightly graying hair and beat-up leather sandals, wrinkled khaki shorts, a pink flamingo shirt, and the grungiest old tennis visor I had ever seen.

"I'm 66 years old," he stated. "Last year I had angioplasty to reduce a 95-percent blockage in a coronary artery and started running so I wouldn't die. I set a goal to break 39 minutes in a 10K and ran 38:50 in the Desert News race. How do I learn to handle the pain I experienced in that race for 26.2 miles?"

John doesn't waste time or words. I learned that, although he had never before run competitively, he had two sons who were college all-American runners. For several months before his fast 10K, John had been training 35 to 50 miles per week, which included an occasional track interval workout and nearly weekly 5K or 10K races. A retired business lawyer, John taught Spanish briefly at the University of Utah while developing a number of hotels at ski resorts in the West. He is a goal-oriented person who is not afraid of challenges and is used to getting what he wants. After setting his 10K PR, he decided he wanted to run his first marathon at St. George in around three hours, an age group course record by nearly an hour. In consecutive weeks he increased his mileage from 50 to 65, and then 75 miles. He called me because instead of feeling faster or stronger, he felt exhausted and completely beat up. He had seven weeks before the marathon, and he wanted some guidance.

Running Smarter, Not Harder

"First, John," I began, "your 10K pace is evidence that you have the potential leg speed to run between 3:03 and 3:10 on the hilly St. George course. But you don't have time to increase your mileage *and* maintain your speed. You will have to be more innovative than to follow some generic training schedule that's not designed to meet the specific needs of this course or your 66-year-old body. Running well in the marathon is not about how hard you can race, but how intelligently you can prepare and how efficiently you can learn to run. Let's do a demonstration."

I asked John to straighten his arm and place his hand, palm up, on my shoulder. As I put my hands on his elbow joint, I told him to try as hard as he could not to let me bend his arm. He took a deep breath, made his body rigid, and grimaced as I easily bent his arm. Then I asked him to shut his eyes, breathe normally, and imagine a rod that came in through his shoulder, inside his upper arm, through his elbow, down his forearm, and out through his fingertips. I waited until he reported that he could clearly see this rod in his mind's eye. As I started to apply pressure, I encouraged him to let go of all other thoughts except the image of this energy rod, which might flex a little but would not bend. With his body relaxed, he focused his energies into the imaginary rod. The harder I pressed down, the more I encouraged him to make the energy rod stiffer. I couldn't bend his arm. He was astonished.

We then discussed how yelling at yourself and urging yourself to try harder is counterproductive, because doing so evokes the idea that you are slowing down and that running is becoming more difficult—and that is exactly what will happen. When John imagined the rod, he focused his energies into his triceps, the only muscles involved in preventing his arm from bending. None of the muscles that tensed the first time in his face, fist, or rigid body were connected to his elbow. Imagery is a much more accurate way to communicate to your body what you want it to do than is overtrying.

Next I asked John to hold his arm out, bend it to 90 degrees at the elbow, make a tight fist, and shake his hand back and forth as fast as he could while maintaining tension in his arm. Then I told him to relax his arm and do the same thing. He was startled at how much faster his arm and hand moved. The same concept applies to running efficiency. Speed is about not just power but the exact amount of energy expended at precisely the right moment in the stride pattern—with minimal tension throughout the rest of your body. Grimacing, tensing your hands and arms, and executing other similar efforts only waste energy.

"So, John," I asked, "how do you run? What do you focus on when the going gets tough?"

"I just grit my teeth and push as hard as I can," he replied. "And that's my problem isn't it?"

During the next several weeks, John and I ran together regularly. At first, John tended to reach with his feet, landing heel first, causing a momentary breaking. Associated with this overstriding, he also overswung his arms out in front of him. Both of these inefficiencies were related to running too upright. Slow-motion video of elite runners showed him that they tended to run with a balanced forward upper body posture, characterized by compact arm swings, soft foot contacts underneath bending knees, and toe-offs well behind their centers of gravity. Within a week or so, John had refined his technique significantly. Before our runs, he often watched one of my videos of elite runners to get a clear image of efficient form. Then he studied videos of himself, contrasting his style with that of the elite runners so that he could identify a new focus objective to improve his technique. While he ran, he not only responded biomechanically to his visualization, but he also learned to feel his body respond to changes in his technique. John was "running younger," with a light, quick, rhythmic, flowing stride. He learned the "Poetry in Motion" verse: "Touch down softly, float over gently, reach back, extend off, fly, fly, fly." He imagined exactly what each phrase meant and ran accordingly. If his form was off, the verse got stuck on the inefficient movement element until he fixed it. John developed an array of psychomechanical skills to develop and maintain efficient running technique for uphills, downhills, flats, and segments when he felt tired.

Preparing for the Race Demands

John's primary training challenge was to prepare for the longer distance without losing his speed. It takes seven to 10 days to get a training effect from a specific workout, so John only had time for two or three long runs before the race. Because the St. George course includes a significant amount of downhill, it was essential that he not lose leg speed, which would happen if he focused primarily on longer runs. He decided to go back to 50 miles per week for the next five weeks and then taper for the last two weeks before the marathon. Because he had already run a 20-miler the previous week, he decided to be creative with his last two long runs.

"How about this weekend I go to St. George," he suggested, "and run the first 15 miles of the course on Saturday morning and the last 15 miles on Sunday morning—finishing both at or near race pace (seven-minute miles)? That way I will have run the whole course at about the same time of the day I will be racing it. Then, if I feel recovered, in three weeks I'll go back down for the St. George 15K, which runs the last part of the marathon course. I'll start earlier at the marathon five- or six-mile mark and try to time my arrival at the 15K to coincide with the start. I'll run the 15K at race pace."

This strategy was a great way to learn the course (environmental demands), to improve his endurance and maintain leg speed (functional demand), to ensure recovery (physical demands), and to practice focusing on technique under race conditions (functional and mental demands). Also, he could stay in the same motel, eat at the same restaurants (logistical demands), and do similar free-time activities (social demands) to what he would do at the actual marathon. He could also determine which shoes and outerwear (technical demands) would be the best and practice drinking the aid (physical demands) that would be available on the race course.

John followed his training plan and even added cold-water soaks and frequent massages to enhance recoveries. On the weeks of his long runs, he reduced his weekday mileage so that he would be fresh enough to run the last part of the long runs at or near race tempo. He also ran a couple of short races and did a few short interval workouts to maintain his speed. His race focus strategy included specific focus objectives for the warm-up, the start, the early miles, the volcano hill, the middle miles, the downhill to Snow Canyon, the long uphill from miles 18 to 20, the crashing downhill to the city limits, and finally the last three miles in town. John planted additional drinks between aid stations so that he could drink immediately if he felt dehydrated or his blood sugar level dropped. His goal was to race each mile as skillfully and efficiently as he could. This goal was totally under his control and left him feeling calm, ready, and cautiously excited about the race.

With a detailed strategy for the skills he would focus on for each segment of the race, with sets of alternative tactics to handle everything he could think of that might happen along the course (blisters, cramps, mother nature calling, etc.), and fully attuned to his body's feedback, John ran 3:04:49 in St. George! Every time he started to lose his focus, he repeated "poetry" until he went back on cruise control. The last miles were tough, but he switched to counting exhales and imagining his way to the finish line. When a reporter asked if he found the race difficult, John answered, "The first 20 miles went by pretty easily, but during the last six miles I made a deal with God: if you pick my feet up, I'll put 'em back down."

By learning to listen to his own body, not getting caught up in "how everybody else trains," and being innovative in his race preparation, John has shown that when old dogs learn new tricks, they can run like young studs. He also learned the benefits of preparing to meet all the demands of the race, not just the training requirements. His left-brain programming took care of getting him to the starting line ready to race. His right brain was effectively programmed to fully express his running skills, abilities, and knowledge. In 1999, John was named Runner of the Year for the 70 to 75 age group by the U.S. Track and Field Association. After a bike accident in which he fractured his hip, lingering tendonitis forced John to switch from running to cycling to strengthen those muscles and connective tissues. In the summer of 2000, he rode his bike from Seattle to Atlantic City in about five weeks. John never does anything halfway. He's now looking forward to continuing to "run younger" as he grows older.

Taking a Structured Approach to Performing

In helping John develop his performance preparation, execution, and assessment strategies, I relied on a structured approach based on what successful elite athletes do. The opportunity to work with world-class age group and elite athletes has reinforced my belief that, although they do have exceptional physical talent, their performance programming skills are the cornerstones of their consistent success. By picking their brains, I developed and refined the performance paradigms and blueprints presented in this book, and I have watched seemingly ordinary athletes use these concepts to perform at extraordinary levels. Dirk Cowley went from being a couch potato in his late 30s to winning the World Masters Stage Race Cycling Championship in Europe in his early 40s by utilizing these principles. Joann Garuccio, five-time World Masters Olympic Distance Triathlon Champion, took up triathlons to help her keep in shape so that she could teach skiing. By applying these principles, she has raced successfully all over the world to win her championships. Dirk and Joann share a simple secret: *proper prior programming promotes "phocused" performances.* They succeeded by developing a structured approach to performing, and so can you!

Preparing to meet the multiple demands of a specific performance involves the following steps:

1. Setting goals

2. Comparing the demands of the race to your current capabilities to identify areas that need improvement

3. Developing specific preparation and execution strategies to improve your skill level and meet race demands

4. Designing a prerace plan to identify potential problems and ways of dealing with them

5. Developing focusing strategies to meet your objectives during the race

6. Assessing the effectiveness of the entire process

These six elements are predominantly left-brain functions. By intimately involving "lefty" in the process through the preparation phases, you significantly improve the probability that "righty" will be in charge during the actual race. The objective is to get to the starting line ready to race, feeling calm, energized, and focused—ready to execute your racing strategies. Let's take a closer look at each of these elements of performance.

Developing specific preparation and execution strategies will get you to the starting line ready to race.

Setting Goals

A race is a process, not just a result. You'll have greater psychological freedom when you develop racing goals based on your overall preparation strategy and training progress. To be effective, your goal should be based on your training achievements and should be something that you can exercise control over before and during the race. You want to motivate your ego to do the training you'll need to raise your performance to that level. The *process statement* outlines what you have to do during the event to achieve your desired results. For example, the process statement, "To race each mile of the course skillfully and efficiently" serves four important functions:

1. It provides direction for your training and preparation, progress markers, and a basis for assessing your overall performance.
2. It commits you to racing the whole course, not just running to finish it.
3. It provides a focus for your attention—application of skills—during the race.
4. It separates your self-worth from the results by focusing on the process from the beginning.

It's the process that is being tested, not you as a person. How well you run the race depends on how well you manage the whole process. If you don't achieve the desired result, it is not because something is wrong with you. It is the process that needs to be modified and refined, not you. On the other hand, a peak performance is truly a celebration of your training. Remember Frank Shorter's comment, "Running fast is more fun than running slow." Set out to have as much *fun* during your race as you can stand!

Finally, keep in mind that initial goals are just that—initial. If your training goes better than expected or other demands restrict your preparation, adjust your goal to be still challenging but attainable. Do not continue to hold onto an ego goal that your body is not prepared to meet. The most satisfying performances are those in which you optimally apply your skills, abilities, and knowledge to meet the demands of the day. So how do I help runners develop challenging but realistic goals? I look at a number of performance predictors.

Predicting Performance

John told me he had run 38:50 on the Desert News 10K for an average pace of 6:15 per mile. Realizing the downhill nature of the course, I adjusted the pace up a bit to come up with a more reasonable predictor of 6:30, which he said was closer to his other 10K race paces. Then I added 30 seconds to this pace and multiplied by 26.2 to estimate the fastest he might expect to run. I did the same with 45 seconds to establish a range of 3:03 to 3:10 for an effective marathon time. This method of establishing a realistic predicted marathon range is quite accurate. You simply add 30 seconds, then 45 seconds, to your most recent 10K pace, and then multiply each by 26.2.

Another method to predict performance is shown in table 6.1. To use this chart, look for your predictor distance in the far left column. Then go across the row and find the ratio under the heading for the distance you want to predict your time for. Take that ratio and multiply it by the reference distance time. For example, if your most recent half-marathon time was 2:00, then your predicted marathon time would be 2:00 × 2.099, or 4:19, over similar terrain and weather conditions. Conversely, if you typically run your better 10Ks in 45 minutes, your potential in a 5K would be 45 minutes × .476, or 21:42 minutes, under similar conditions.

TABLE 6.1 Performance Predictor

	Mile	5K	10K	Half marathon	Marathon
Mile	1.000	3.630	7.061	15.697	32.955
5K	.297	1.000	2.099	4.667	9.798
10K	.142	.476	1.000	2.223	4.667
Half marathon	.064	.214	.450	1.000	2.099
Marathon	.030	.102	.214	.476	1.000

Reprinted, by permission, from P. Riegel, 1981, *American Scientist* May–June.

I also find the following techniques useful for ballpark predictions:

2 × your 5K time + 1 minute = your estimated 10K time.

2 × your half-marathon time + 10 minutes = a solid predictor for your marathon time.

2.1 × your half-marathon time = another accurate projection for your marathon time.

Finally, there are Bart Yasso's 800s. Bart, who is a *Runner's World* staffer, has observed that you can predict your marathon time by determining the average time for ten consecutive 800s (two laps around a track) with the same amount of rest between each. For example, we were not surprised when John ran his 3:05 marathon at age 73, because he had built up his repeat 800s to about 95 seconds (three minutes and five seconds, or 3:05) with 95 seconds of rest between 800s.

One of the ways I found to keep myself and my runners motivated over the years is to calculate comparable performance times. Early in my career, I recognized that one of the reasons I would never be a world-champion runner was that I didn't possess the body for it. Back then, a weight-to-height ratio of 2 pounds per inch of height for men and 1.7 pounds per inch of height for women were considered ideal for distance runners. As I grew older, it was obvious to me that age is also a factor in running performance. So the scheming scientist in me set out to develop a way of adjusting my times based on my age and weight-to-height ratio to a comparable time for a skinny young stud. By manipulating the formula for kinetic energy (KE = mass/2 × velocity^2), I calculated a factor adjust for weight-to-height ratios. Using tables from a now-ancient booklet ("Racing Techniques," *Runners World* Publications, 1972), I developed factors to reflect the decline in performance based on age.

Table 6.2 combines these features and can be used in a number of ways. At this year's Las Vegas half-marathon, John ran 1:40:12. He is 69 inches tall and weighs 138 pounds, so his ratio is 2.0. Go down the 2.0 column to the bottom. At almost 77, he's off the page, so extrapolate to .64 and multiply it by his time to

TABLE 6.2   Comparable Performance Tables

Men

Age/Wt: Ht ratio	2.00	2.10	2.20	2.30	2.40	2.50	2.60	2.70	2.80	2.90	3.00
15–20 yrs	.94	.92	.89	.87	.86	.84	.83	.81	.79	.78	.77
21–25	.97	.95	.92	.90	.88	.86	.85	.83	.82	.81	.80
26–30	1.00	.98	.95	.93	.91	.89	.88	.86	.84	.83	.82
31–35	.98	.96	.93	.91	.89	.87	.86	.84	.82	.81	.80
36–40	.95	.93	.90	.88	.86	.85	.84	.82	.80	.79	.78
41–45	.92	.90	.87	.86	.84	.82	.81	.79	.77	.76	.75
46–50	.88	.86	.84	.82	.80	.78	.77	.76	.74	.73	.72
51–55	.84	.82	.80	.78	.76	.75	.74	.72	.71	.70	.69
56–60	.79	.77	.75	.73	.72	.71	.70	.68	.66	.65	.64
61–65	.75	.73	.71	.70	.68	.67	.66	.65	.63	.62	.61
66–70	.70	.69	.67	.65	.64	.62	.61	.60	.59	.58	.57

Women

Age/Wt: Ht ratio	1.70	1.80	1.90	2.00	2.10	2.20	2.30	2.40	2.50
15–20 yrs	.94	.91	.88	.86	.85	.83	.81	.79	.77
21–25	.97	.94	.91	.89	.87	.85	.83	.81	.80
26–30	1.00	.97	.94	.92	.90	.88	.86	.84	.82
31–35	.98	.95	.92	.90	.88	.86	.84	.82	.80
36–40	.95	.92	.89	.87	.86	.84	.82	.80	.78
41–45	.92	.89	.86	.85	.83	.81	.79	.77	.75
46–50	.88	.85	.83	.81	.79	.77	.76	.74	.72
51–55	.84	.81	.79	.77	.76	.74	.72	.71	.69
56–60	.79	.77	.74	.73	.71	.70	.68	.66	.65
61–65	.75	.73	.71	.69	.68	.66	.65	.63	.62
66–70	.70	.68	.66	.64	.63	.62	.60	.59	.57

Reference: *Racing Techniques:* Runner's World *Booklet of the Month,* 1972 (July).

get 1:04:08. Both times are nearly world class, so the comparison is reasonable. Or how about comparing my time in last weekend's Moab 5-miler to Mike Evan's. At 58 years, 65 inches, and 165 pounds (wt ÷ ht = 2.54), I have a comparable factor of about .705. Converted to a comparable time for a skinny 26- to 30-year-old, my time is 38:12 × .705 = 26.87. Mike, at 26 years old, 70 inches, and 140 pounds, is already optimum and gets no break. His factor is 1.0. So his second place finish in 25:51 stands, but I wasn't far behind—"comparably." This conversion is what keeps old dogs like me running. If you're mathematically inclined, you can use the table to compare current and past performances of your own. You will probably be surprised at the consistency of your adjusted times.

Establishing Challenging yet Realistic Goals

The point of this discussion is to enable you to set realistic goals. If you're unable to come up with reliable results using at least one of these methods, you have two choices, depending on how much time is left before the race. If time is short, adjust your desired result downward. If you have time to improve at the shorter distances, work on that aspect of your training. The will to prepare is the mark of the champion. When your progress markers (in the form of results from shorter races) support your desired longer distance goals, you will arrive at the start more confident in your skills and abilities and ready to focus on your running.

Assessing the Demands of the Race

Carefully analyzing the demands for a specific event will reveal areas where you must improve to meet your desired goal. A systematic approach reduces careless error. The most common error is to focus exclusively on the specific physical demands of an event. For example, let's say you're getting ready for a marathon and you decide to focus all of your energy on improving your endurance. By focusing on this one aspect, you have forgotten all of the other factors that influence your performance. In focusing only on endurance, you may

- neglect leg speed,
- forget to register early and reserve a place to stay,

- show up in racing flats in which you have never done a long run,

- neglect to train with the same drinks that will be on the course, or

- not realize that there is a long uphill or downhill at a critical point in the race.

These are just a few things that, if not accounted for, can seriously inhibit your performance!

Functional Demands

Functional demands are requirements that are specific to a given event. In John's case, the functional demands were holding form and maintaining leg speed during the final six miles of steep-to-gradual downhill to the finish after a challenging 20 miles. For Harry and me in the World Blind Marathon Championship, racing two marathons within two weeks was a functional challenge. Running in Boston or New York requires you to run in an urban setting with a huge crowd looking on, as opposed to the mostly high desert, solitary environment of St. George. I use the term *functional* because it refers to any kind of performing situation. Auditioning for an acting, singing, or musical position; taking college entrance exams or tests in school; making a pitch to raise money for a pet project; speaking in public; or taking your driver's test are examples of everyday functional demands.

Physical Demands

Physical demands relate to general health, fitness, rest, nutrition, and hydration. If long drives or flights are involved in getting to an event, how much rest and recovery time will you need to be ready to go on race day? If you are going to increase your volume of training, you must be able to increase the amount of sleep you can get proportionately. World-class runner Doug Padilla told a running camp audience that the secret of his longevity was basing his volume of training on how much time he had to sleep, not train. Tapering strategies that allow you to recover from your training and leave you energized reflect physical demands. If you rarely do much walking and standing around, spending all day at the "Expo" the day before a race will leave you stiff the next day.

Watch out for common physical mistakes, such as forgetting to stay hydrated and to maintain intensity while you reduce the volume of training during tapering. Your physical goal is to arrive at the starting line fully prepared, rested, and energized to meet the demands of the course.

To effectively train for a race, it's important to develop training runs that simulate the terrain demands of the course.

Mental and Emotional Demands

Mental and emotional demands are intimately connected. Although the media and many athletes and coaches claim that competing is mostly mental, I'm not sure I agree. In my own best performances and those of the athletes with whom I have worked closely, the intellectual part was in developing the detailed preparation. The events themselves seemed to happen automatically—with little conscious thinking or emotion—as though the left brain was only observing while the right brain took over.

The key seems to lie in developing ways to manage your emotions before and during an event. How you assess the situation determines your mental and emotional set. For the most part, *emotion* is a cognitive (thinking) response to a situation. Statements such as, "If I don't make the Olympic team, I will have wasted four years of my life," are ineffective situational assessments that can lead to inhibited performances. When you feel the emotional rush instigated by your ego's demands, refocus from the desired outcome or failure to what you can control—what you are doing at the moment. The key to emotion/critic management is attention control. Your clumsy left-brain programmer can only handle one verbal task at a time, so direct your left brain to execute audiogenics, counting, or some other activity that will not interfere with your skilled right-brain programmer's ability to execute your performance strategies. Remember, emotions short-circuit your brain and allow ego viruses to disrupt your performance programming.

Social and Logistical Demands

The social part deals with such issues as who will go with you; what they will do before, during, and after the event; and how they will deal with your nervousness before the big race. Logistics include race registration, lodging, meals, transportation, and shopping for specific food, gear, or equipment—money-related issues. World-champion triathlete Joann Garuccio often secures her plane and lodging reservations for a foreign race as much as six months in advance so that she doesn't have to worry about it at the last minute. Plus, making logistical arrangements deepens her commitment to train and prepare.

Environmental and Technical Demands

Environmental and technical demands also go together. Should you run in racing flats or training shoes on a hilly course? Is a T-shirt, a singlet, or long sleeves more appropriate? What if it rains, or is hot, or both? You must consider not only the terrain demands, which are constant, but also the weather, which can be highly variable, and prepare to meet all potential conditions. If you can't run on the racecourse, research and develop training runs that simulate the racecourse's terrain demands. Olympic cross-country skiing silver medallist and World Cup champion Bill Koch was reported to have summer cycling courses that reflected the skiing terrain demands of all the World Cup courses. Your preparation to meet the course demands of your races is limited only by the extent of your imagination.

Developing Specific Preparation and Execution Strategies

Once you have carefully analyzed the array of specific demands of your big race, it's time to start planning—backward! To help you begin your backward performance programming, refer to figure 6.1, a sample Prerace Planning Guide. After you answer the questions it asks, you'll write your answers in the bull's-eye area of the Performance Programming Target (see the sample in figure 6.2). The Performance Programming Target is divided into four quadrants, one for each of the pairs of performance demands. The rings represent timeframes starting at the performance itself—the bull's-eye that you are aiming for. The next ring represents the time you spend on-site for the event, while the third ring depicts the time you spend doing event-specific training. The outermost portion in each quadrant is for planning regular training and preparation strategies. Notice that the area within each ring decreases as time gets closer to the performance. If you have programmed well, by the time you arrive at the starting line, all you have to focus on is racing—skillfully and efficiently. You are calm, focused, and energized.

Take a look at the sample Prerace Planning Guide and Performance Programming Target (figures 6.1 and 6.2), and then try your hand at creating your own in the blank forms provided (figures 6.3 and 6.4). Feel free to make copies of the worksheets so that you can plan properly before every race.

FIGURE 6.1   Sample Prerace Planning Guide

Event: *Sugarhouse Park 5K time trial*   **Date:** *June 20*

Desired result: *Sub 21:42*

Goal statement: *Race each mile as skillfully and efficiently as possible, taking full advantage of downhill segments, not going anaerobic on uphills, and focusing on balanced forward posture, compact arm swing, pelvic tilt, and turnover rate.*

Course description (segmented by physical and/or technique demand changes): *Two-plus laps of rolling hills on smooth pavements. First mile includes a gentle downhill for the first couple of minutes, a flat section followed by a steep short uphill, a short flat, and a gentle downhill to the mile marker. Second mile starts flat, followed by a short abrupt uphill, then longer gentle downhill to short drop, then flat to start of uphill. Third mile continues uphill to flat, gentle down, flat, abrupt up, and gentle downhill to finish. Course demands solid uphill/ downhill running skills.*

How will you optimize your skills to get the most speed out of this course? *Effective warm-up is essential and must include uphill/downhill striding. On downs, must control speed with body posture while focusing on quick, compact arm swings and not reaching with feet. Overbreathe just before uphills and then maintain constant race effort by adjusting posture, turnover rate, and/or stride length. Run "light and quick, forward, forward" on the flats.*

How do you want to feel physically, mentally, and emotionally at the start? *Calm, focused, charged, "ready"—mentally. Loose, relaxed, warmed up—physically.*

At race time, what environmental/technical and social/logistical factors must you consider? *Site is only minutes from home, so weather will be known and appropriate dress/ shoes obvious. Have bottle of sports drink at start and drink about 10 to 12 ounces just before start. Have another bottle of sports drink for after. Ask running group if anyone wants to participate and agree on start time.*

What can go wrong, and how will you handle each situation?

- *Need to go to bathroom (again) immediately before start—run across street to fast food restaurant.*
- *Didn't warm up and stretch enough, feel stiff at start—focus on running relaxed, visualize skeleton running perfectly, ease off until rhythm is established.*
- *Blister, trip and fall, windier than expected, having a bad day—"shut up and run," manage everything that comes up.*

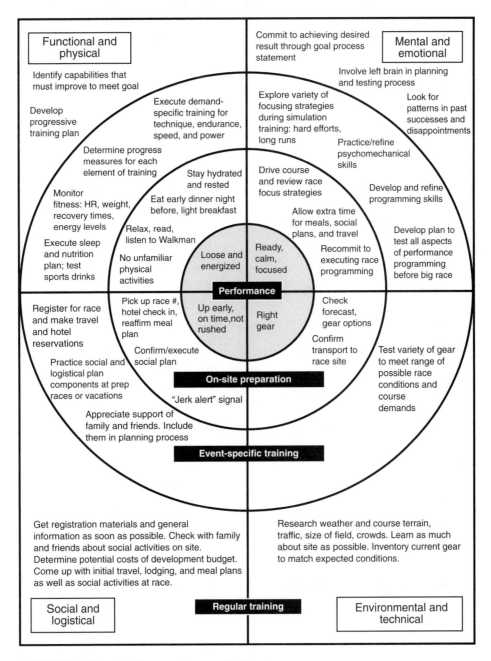

FIGURE 6.2   Sample Performance Programming Target.

FIGURE 6.3 Prerace Planning Guide

Event: Date:

Desired result:

Goal statement:

Course description (segmented by physical and/or technique demand changes):

How will you optimize your skills to get the most speed out of this course?

How do you want to feel physically, mentally, and emotionally at the start?

At race time, what environmental/technical and social/logistical factors must you consider?

What can go wrong, and how will you handle each situation?

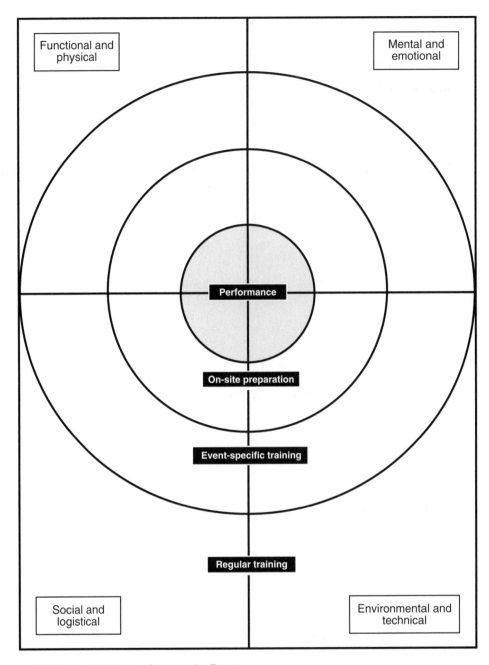

FIGURE 6.4   Performance Programming Target.

The purpose of these exercises is to raise your capabilities in each area to the level required to meet your performance goal. Let's now look at what to do once you are at the event site.

Designing a Prerace Plan

This segment of the programming process covers the time from the end of your event-specific training and preparation until the start of the event. Most of us experience nervousness and anxiety as we get closer to the event. Identifying what you are worrying about, writing it down, and then developing a way of dealing with the problem(s) or issue(s) is incredibly helpful in managing your mind. Use the Prerace Plan in figure 6.5 for this purpose. It is most useful when you fill it out a day or so before the race and then amend it as necessary as the time gets closer. This process is another form of left-brain management—keep that sucker busy or, given nothing to do, it will look for things to worry about. This concept brings us to the last element of our performance programming.

Developing Focusing Strategies

There's an old saying, "You can't eat an elephant in one bite." For runners I suggest a modification: "You can't run a race with one step." The basic truth is the same. To optimize your overall performance, you need to manage each step along the way to the best of your ability. Consistently successful athletes have more effective focusing strategies to keep them "in the moment" and attentive to the task at hand. The more important the race, the more important it is for you to segment the course with respect to the physical and mental demands of each section.

Remember the strategies Harry and I developed for Boston and the World Blind Marathon Championship? In each case, we had an intimate knowledge of not only the terrain demands but also the psychological demands, such as crowded starts, rough pavement, screaming crowds, etc. We developed focus plans in which we controlled our attention. If our minds wandered, we could return to the plan. Starts, uphills, downhills, wind, weather, crowds, bathroom stops, cramps, and dehydration are just some of the factors that you need to prepare to handle. After running marathons for years, Jim Doilney set a PR in the marathon at age

FIGURE 6.5   Prerace Plan

Day before race (objectives—what you want to accomplish in each demand area):

- Functional/physical:

- Mental/emotional:

- Social/logistical:

- Environmental/technical:

Prior to sleep (objectives/plan):

Wakeup to departure for race (objectives/plan):

Travel to race site (objectives/plan):

Arrival until warm-up (objectives/plan):

Warm-up (objectives/plan):

Prestart (moments before start—objectives/plan):

50. He went so far as to write focus cues on the water bottles that he set out at critical places on the course. His reminders included "steady effort, chop the uphills," "spin 'em" on the downhills, and "swing 'em and breathe" in the later miles.

Engage your left brain intimately in developing *how and what you are going to think about* (attention control) during each section of the race. Mentally rehearse the run. Simulate conditions during training to practice and refine your skills. Come race day, you'll arrive at the starting line ready to race!

Assessing the Effectiveness of Your Preparation Strategies

Because a performance is a process, not just a result, performers can benefit from a structured assessment tool. The Performance Programming Assessment presented in figure 6.6 is designed to be partially filled out the night before the race and fully completed after the race. By now the concepts in the Performance Programming Assessment are familiar to you. Answer questions 1 through 4 to review your training and preparation in each area, account for any unexpected development that might effect the outcome of the event, review your racing strategies, and recommit to your tactics to handle your emotions/inner critic before and during the event. Once all the questions are addressed, most athletes have little trouble sleeping and wake up ready to race! Working through the questions is exactly the process that Harry and I went through to get back on track for the world championships.

Questions 5 through 18 deal with the effectiveness of your performance programming in each area of preparation. You are asked to rate your effectiveness for each item on a scale from one to 10. These items reflect all of the concepts discussed and illustrated throughout this book. By making copies of this clean assessment and then judiciously using them in your racing, you can become your own head coach. The final section allows you to score your performance on some 25 elements, only two of which deal specifically with the degree to which you achieved your goal statement and desired result. In other words, you can use the scoring to identify your performing strengths and weaknesses with respect to your preparation strategies, your ability to maintain an effective performance state of mind, and your concentration/attention control.

FIGURE 6.6 Performance Programming Assessment

Complete <u>underlined items</u> (1–4) *prior* to performance; others after performance.

Event: **Date:**

Desired goal: **Actual result:**

Process goal statement:

Prerace Strategies

1. <u>Describe your preparation, testing and refinement strategies to meet these demands:</u>

   Functional (event specific skills, abilities, and knowledge);

   Physical (fitness, nutrition, hydration, and rest):

   Mental/emotional (arousal, attention, emotion, and internal critic management and control):

   Environmental/technical (matching equipment, gear, and clothing with surroundings):

   Social/logistical (registration, travel, lodging, meals, and social support plan before and during event):

2. <u>Describe any unanticipated situations that developed before the event that affected your preparation or training:</u>

(continued)

3. Describe your segment focus objectives for each part of your performance:

Up to 30 minutes before the start:

Warm-up (30 minutes until prestart)**:**

Prestart (Moments before the start)**:**

Start:

Early parts:

Middle parts:

Last parts:

Finish:

4. What is your strategy to manage your emotions and internal critic before and during this event?

(continued)

Postevent Assessment

5. Rate your preparation strategies in each area from 0 (disaster) to 10 (totally effective):

Functional   0 1 2 3 4 5 6 7 8 9 10

Physical   0 1 2 3 4 5 6 7 8 9 10

Mental/emotional   0 1 2 3 4 5 6 7 8 9 10

Environmental/technical   0 1 2 3 4 5 6 7 8 9 10

Social/logistical   0 1 2 3 4 5 6 7 8 9 10

6. What changes should you have made to your preparation, and why?

7. Rate your mental/emotional state going into this event:

Threatened/scared	0 1 2 3 4 5 6 7 8 9 10	Challenged
Worried/doubtful	0 1 2 3 4 5 6 7 8 9 10	Confident
Result-focused	0 1 2 3 4 5 6 7 8 9 10	Task-focused
Mental chatter	0 1 2 3 4 5 6 7 8 9 10	Calm/ready
Physically tight	0 1 2 3 4 5 6 7 8 9 10	Loose/relaxed
Listless/tired	0 1 2 3 4 5 6 7 8 9 10	Energized
Emotional/bummed out	0 1 2 3 4 5 6 7 8 9 10	Excited
Self-critical	0 1 2 3 4 5 6 7 8 9 10	Totally prepared

8. Identify any factors that influenced very low or high mental/emotional states scores and what you can do to better manage the low scoring items and repeat highs.

9. Rate the effectiveness of your segment concentration from 0 (totally ineffective) to 10 (totally effective).

Up to 30 minutes before start   0 1 2 3 4 5 6 7 8 9 10

Warm-up   0 1 2 3 4 5 6 7 8 9 10

Prestart   0 1 2 3 4 5 6 7 8 9 10

Start   0 1 2 3 4 5 6 7 8 9 10

Early Parts   0 1 2 3 4 5 6 7 8 9 10

Middle Parts   0 1 2 3 4 5 6 7 8 9 10

Last Parts   0 1 2 3 4 5 6 7 8 9 10

Finish   0 1 2 3 4 5 6 7 8 9 10

(continued)

10. Describe any situation before or during the event when you felt exceptionally effective or ineffective.

11. Rate your ability to manage your effort during this event.

    Lost it/blew up   0 1 2 3 4 5 6 7 8 9 10   Maintained throughout

12. What was going on in your head when you were at your highest intensity level?

13. How focused were you during this event?

    Wandering mind   0 1 2 3 4 5 6 7 8 9 10   Completely absorbed

14. What was going on in your head when you were performing well?

15. How well did you manage your emotions/internal critic before and during this event?

    Constant self-criticism/turmoil   0 1 2 3 4 5 6 7 8 9 10   Calm/focused

16. To what degree were you able to execute your goal statement?

    Completely lost it   0 1 2 3 4 5 6 7 8 9 10   Held it together

17. Performance rating based on time, place, score—outcome.

    Failure   0 1 2 3 4 5 6 7 8 9 10   Outstanding

18. What did you learn from this competition that will help you improve your next performance?

(continued)

Scoring

Preparation

Functional	0 1 2 3 4 5 6 7 8 9 10
Physical	0 1 2 3 4 5 6 7 8 9 10
Mental/emotional	0 1 2 3 4 5 6 7 8 9 10
Environmental/technical	0 1 2 3 4 5 6 7 8 9 10
Social/logistical	0 1 2 3 4 5 6 7 8 9 10
Total preparation	___ / 50

Pre-event performance state

Feeling threatened or challenged	0 1 2 3 4 5 6 7 8 9 10
Feeling worried or confident at the start	0 1 2 3 4 5 6 7 8 9 10
Focused on results or task at start	0 1 2 3 4 5 6 7 8 9 10
Mind full of chatter or calm before start	0 1 2 3 4 5 6 7 8 9 10
Physically tight or loose and relaxed at start	0 1 2 3 4 5 6 7 8 9 10
Feeling tired or energized at the start	0 1 2 3 4 5 6 7 8 9 10
Distracted by emotion or excitedly focused	0 1 2 3 4 5 6 7 8 9 10
Down on yourself or totally ready to go	0 1 2 3 4 5 6 7 8 9 10
Total pre-event performance state	___ / 80

(continued)

Race concentration

Perceived effectiveness up 30 minutes before start	0 1 2 3 4 5 6 7 8 9 10
Warm-up	0 1 2 3 4 5 6 7 8 9 10
Prestart	0 1 2 3 4 5 6 7 8 9 10
Start	0 1 2 3 4 5 6 7 8 9 10
Early Parts	0 1 2 3 4 5 6 7 8 9 10
Middle Parts	0 1 2 3 4 5 6 7 8 9 10
Last Parts	0 1 2 3 4 5 6 7 8 9 10
Finish	0 1 2 3 4 5 6 7 8 9 10
Managing effort during event	0 1 2 3 4 5 6 7 8 9 10
Attentional control during event	0 1 2 3 4 5 6 7 8 9 10
Emotional and critic management	0 1 2 3 4 5 6 7 8 9 10
Total concentration	___ / 110

Results

Process goal statement achievement	0 1 2 3 4 5 6 7 8 9 10
Results based on time, place, score, etc.	0 1 2 3 4 5 6 7 8 9 10
Total results	___ / 20

Total score   ___/260

Ordinary to Extraordinary

I've worked with several elite athletes in sports that I have very limited firsthand experience of. They have taken the assessment tools in this chapter and virtually coached themselves to higher levels of performance—as high as the U.S. Olympic team. To end this lesson and the book, I have chosen to include this article on some very special runners.

During an easy morning run, Debbie Moss said, "This weekend will be my last long run before the race in three weeks. How long should I go—two, three hours—what do you think?" Jokingly, I responded, "Why not eight hours?" Debbie fired back, "Eight hours! Tom, the race is only a 50-miler." We both erupted in laughter at the irony of her statement.

Several years earlier, Debbie had joined our running group. She had recently gone through a divorce, was now a single mom with two young daughters, and was about to face getting back into the job market. Running helped her cope with stress.

My first impression was that she was a quiet, slender woman of ordinary physical gifts. She responded well to both my technique-centered coaching and the social support of the group. Deb became a regular at our Tuesday and Thursday workouts. Soon she was thrilled to be finishing 5K and 10K races, even though her times were not very fast. She had even completed the challenging Wasatch Steeplechase trail race.

After one workout, Debbie asked if we could talk. She had just signed up for a refresher program in nursing and was scared she would fail. It had been several years since she had worked as a nurse, and all the classes were really tough. I asked her how she had approached the Steeplechase Race, a tough 16-mile trail run. She answered, "One section at a time," and then smiled and said, "That's how I'll get through the refresher course: focus on one class at a time!" Deb and her daughters also discussed how she needed their help to meet her studying, running, and "mommying" demands. A couple of weeks later, Debbie came to running group with a huge smile on her face. She had aced her first class. She finished the refresher course with straight As and got a full-time nursing position.

With the help of her new husband, Lee, a burn-unit nurse and one-man support team, Debbie started running marathons. With an eye toward attempting the JFK 50-miler, Debbie upped her mileage and speed work and suffered a stress fracture. As she was recovering, she devised a new training approach that was suited to her own physiology. Debbie calls her approach "tweak management." After a long, hard, or fast run or race, she doesn't do another one until she feels fresh and eager again. Not only does she get a better training effect this way, but she also has more time to meet all the other demands in her busy life.

After successfully finishing the JFK, Debbie entered the 100-mile Western States Endurance Run. Using tweak management, she prepared for the 100 by running two road marathons and the American River 50, with a month between each race. The month before the 100, she ran a trail marathon. During each race Deb practiced her hydration and eating strategies for the 100 and ran at her regular training pace while checking out which shoes and gear to wear under different conditions. After each race she rode her bike and ran at an easy pace for short distances until she felt good again before resuming regular training. She measured her training progress not by miles but rather by how she felt during each race, whether she could maintain her pace throughout the race, and how quickly she recovered. To prepare for the demands of the 100, during the last month before the race Debbie replaced her longer runs with long, hard hikes with Lee. At 42, she finished this grueling race with a smile on her face and her head held high. With the help of her supportive family, Debbie has learned to balance her family life, professional demands, and training while partnering her mind and body to find extraordinary success with her ordinary talent.

Although I have a doctorate in human performance, many of my more profound insights in this area have come from working with real people, like Debbie, who have full-time jobs, families, and responsibilities, as they discover themselves through sports. Several other runners provide inspiring examples.

Two more athletes whom I have watched become elites in their sports are Joann Garuccio and Debbie Wagner. Jo is a four-time consecutive age-group world triathlon masters champion at the Olympic distances. Debbie has won several Ride and Tie World Championships (with either her husband, David, or her daughter, Wendy), the Pikes Peak and St. George Marathons, and the Wasatch Front 100 Mile Endurance Run, and she is an elite masters cross-country skier. Both Debbie and Jo train and prepare for competition with the intelligence of scientists so that they can race like animals. When they arrive at the starting line, they know exactly what they will focus on during each segment of the race and they're confident that all their equipment and gear has been tested and is ready to go. Their rational minds have explored everything that might happen before or during the race, and they have practiced

strategies to resolve these issues effectively. The goal is always to manage everything that comes up creatively and effectively so that, regardless of the time or place at the finish, they know they put in their best effort. For example, a few years ago, before the Ride and Tie World Championship at a hot, steamy course in California, Debbie had a flash of brilliance and said to her husband and daughter, "Let's shave the horse so that he'll stay cooler!" They won—again.

Perhaps my favorite teachers are the running grandmothers in my group. Linda "Hooper" Wahlquist and Ina Smith have run with me for years. Edie Schiesser joined the group a couple of years ago. Hooper discovered that by telling her critic, "Shut up," and refocusing on her form she could qualify for the Boston Marathon—several times. Ina always worried about what people would say if she didn't finish the marathon. After several slow marathons she became determined to go for it. This time she prepared by doing her long runs at her goal pace and concentrating on her form. As Ina came by the 18-mile mark at St. George, she was radiant. She went on to a personal best by some 20 minutes. Then, there is Edie. Quiet and a little shy at first, she is discovering the empowerment of speed and strength training. At times, "Speedy Edie" surprises herself by her newfound aggressiveness and tenacity, which bloom on tougher trail runs. No longer satisfied with shorter road races, Edie is aiming at longer trail runs.

You, too, can achieve extraordinary successes in your life when you apply the same elements of process focusing and performance programming that these ordinary people have learned, refined, and demonstrated.

Summary

The key to reaching your performance potential lies in smart planning:

- Do the required training, refine your running technique, and learn what to focus on to run efficiently.
- Plan and prepare imaginatively to meet not only the physical demands of the race but also the mental, emotional, functional, social, logistical, environmental, and technical requirements—and test your solutions in training and practice races.
- Base your race goals on your training progress. Don't expect to set a PR at a longer distance if you are not also faster at shorter distances.
- Break the race down into short, manageable segments, each with its own focus objectives. Meeting early segment objectives builds confidence for later sections.
- During the race, focus on the things that you have control over: tensionless effort, stride length and frequency, arm swing, foot plant and push-off, audiogenics, imaging, hydration/nutrition, balanced posture, breathing, and blood sugar management.
- Replace negative self-talk with positive, image-enhancing, energizing words, or, when you're really tired, simply count your exhales.
- Become your own best training partner and friend, and talk to yourself accordingly—cheer for yourself, console yourself, and celebrate with yourself.
- Remind yourself that running is something you do, not who you are. A disappointing performance means only that you need to work on your preparation and execution strategies; it is not a reflection of your self-worth.
- Know that you are already special because there never was or will be another just like you!

Gotta run,

Tom

Bibliography

Anderson, O. 1993. Recover during hard training and race faster with the "Miller Method." *Running Research News* 9 (5): 1–4.

———. 1994a. Running economy, anthropometric dimensions, and kinematic variables. *Medicine and Science in Sports and Exercise* 26 (5): 170.

———. 1994b. Tall in the saddle. *Runner's World* (June) 96–97.

———. 1997a. Be a better runner without higher fitness—with the right form (Part I). *Running Research News* 13 (1): 1, 6–8.

———. 1997b. Form II: What you've gotta do. *Running Research News* 13 (3): 6–8.

Bloom, M. 2001. Back to the future. *Runner's World* (April) 50.

Bowerman, B., and G. Brown. 1971. Secrets of Speed. *Sports Illustrated* (August) 22–27.

Bramble, D.M., and D.R. Carrier. 1983. Running and breathing in mammals. *Science* 219:251–256.

Burfoot, A. 1986. Screen tests. Written from research compiled by D. Buckalew et al. *Runner's World* (March) 48–49.

Cerutty, P. 1960. *Athletics*. London: The Sportsmans Club.

Costill, D. 1986. *Inside Running: Basics of Sports Physiology*. Indianapolis: Benchmark Press.

Costill, D., and G. Branham. How Clayton measures up. *Runner's World*.

Galloway, J. 1984. *Galloway's Book on Running*. Bolinas, CA: Shelter Publications.

———. 1999. Easy glider. *Runner's World* (November) 48.

Garfield, C. 1984. *Peak Performance*. New York: Warner Books.

Hamilton, N. 1993. Changes in sprint stride kinematics with age in master's athletes. *Journal of Applied Biomechanics* 9: 15–26.

Johnson, B. 1997. Speed master. *Running Times* (June) 25–30.

Johnson, D.W. 1981. *Reaching Out*. Englewood Cliffs, NJ: Prentice Hall Inc.

Kuehls, D. 1999. Moving up. *Runner's World* (October) 90–91.

McKay, M., and P. Fanning. 1987. *Self Esteem*. Oakland, CA: New Harbinger Publications.

Paavolainen, L., K. Hakkinen, I. Hamalainen, A. Nummela, and H.U. Rusko. 1999. Explosive strength training improves 5-km running time by improving running economy and muscle power. *Journal of Applied Physiology* 86 (5): 1527–33.

[No author listed]. *Racing Techniques.* 1972. Runner's World *Booklet of the Month* (July) 41–43.

Rono, H. 1979. *The Runner.* (34).

Schechter, B. 1999. How much higher? How much faster? *Scientific American* 11 (3): 11.

Unestahl, L. 1983. *The Mental Aspects of Sports.* Salt Lake City: Vese Publishing.

Wilmore, J., and D. Costill. 1999. *Physiology of Sport and Exercise.* Champaign, IL: Human Kinetics.

Wilt, F. 1964. *Run, Run, Run.* Los Altos, CA: Track and Field News.

Zachariassen, __. 1990. Talk test. *Runners World* (May) 11.

Index

Note: The italicized *f* and *t* following page numbers refer to figures and tables, respectively. **Bold** page references refer to photographs.

A

altitude 45
Anderson, Owen 32
anxiety 95-97, 104, 108
arm action **26, 27,** 32, 33, 39-40, 55-57, 67
arousal 103-104
assessment, of current technique 48-50
assumptions, abandoning 20
attitude 104, 106
audiogenics 54-55, 56, 62, 89-90
"Avenues" workout 69
Ayers, J.W. 2

B

balanced forward posture 31-32, **34**-37, **35, 36**
Barsosio, Sally 34, **35**
belly breathing 5, 41-45
biofeedback, using 52, 63, 77, 87, 120
blind runners 14-20
blood volume 72
Bloom, M. 32
Boston Marathon 7-10, 16-17
Bowerman, B. 41
brain's hemispheric functioning 11-14, 84-87, 88-90, 99, 106
Bramble, D.M. 44
Branham, George 23
breathing skills 40-45
Brown, G. 41
Buckalew, 28

C

Cahill, John 118-123
Camp Smith (Hawaii) 5
carbon dioxide 42
Carrier, D.R. 44
Cerutty, Percy 5
characterological self-esteem 95
Clayton, Derek 23-24
climbing hills 40, 73
comparable performance tables 127-129, 128*t*
Cordellos, Harry 14-20, **15**
Costill, David 23, 30, 39, 42
Cowley, Dick 123
critic management 92-97
cross-training (cycling) 70-71, 75
cycling as training method 70-71, 75

D

descriptive words 52, 54-55, 56
distractions, overcoming 10
Doilney, Jim 138-140
downhill training 67
drive phase (stride) 25, **26, 27,** 29

E

"Easy Glider" 31-32
ego 104
elbow bend 32, 49
elite runners
    critic management by 94-95
    efficiency 23-24
    running mechanics of 5, 7

emotion management 92-97, 106, 132
endurance training 71-73
energy sources, supplementary 38-40
environmental demands assessment 133, 135*f*
evaluation, postevent 114-115, 140, 143*f,* 144*f,* 145*f,* 146*f*
Evans, Mike 36-**37**
event demands assessment 129-130
exercise physiology 11
exhalation 42-45
"Explosive Strength Training Improves 5-Km Running Time by Improving Running Economy and Muscle Power" 68

F

Faerber, Johnny 5
Fanning, P. 95
fartlek 73
femur position 30
"firing" 52
"flying" 52
focused breathing 41
focusing, mental 9-14, 138-140
foot plant **26,** 33, 49
form, running. *See* posture
frequency, stride 28-30, 66-67
functional demands assessment 130, 135*f*

G

Galloway, Jeff 31-32
Galloway's Book on Running 31
Garuccio, Joann 123, 132, 148
glycogen stores 45
goals 109-110, 113-114, 125-129, 126*t,* 128*t*

H

Hakkinen, K. 68

Hamalainen, I. 68
Hamilton, N. 29
hamstrings 29-30
Harness, Swing-Rite 55-**58**
Harper, Sheryl **50**
Hawaii 5, 7
hill climbing 4073
"How Clayton Measures Up" 23-24

I

identity, and running 92-97, 109-112
imagery 54-55, 76
inefficiencies, common 49
intervals, track 61-64, 73

J

Johnson, Brooks 30
Johnson, D.W. 112
Jow, Tom **36**

K

Kenyan runners 34-37
kinesthetic awareness 52, 63, 77, 87, 108
Kipkiter, Sammy **34**-35
Kuehls, David 38

L

Larson, Olle 55
lean. *See* posture
levering off 29-30
"loading" 52
logistical demands assessment 132, 135*f*
Lydiard, Arthur 5

M

marathon preparation 118-123, 126
Marine Corps Physical Fitness Test (PFT) 5-7
Marquette University 3
McKay, M. 95

mental demands assessment 132, 135*f*

mental focusing 9-14, 138-140. *See also* psychomechanics

mileage amounts 71-73

Miller, Thomas S.
early racing career 7
first Boston Marathon 7-10
first marathon 3-4
with Harry Cordellos 14-20, **15**
and John Cahill 118-123
at University of Utah 11-14
in Vietnam 4-5

Milwaukee Marathon 3-4

Moss, Debbie 36-**37**, 147-148

"Moving Up" 38

muscles, elasticity of 38-40

N

Naval Enlisted Scientific Education Program (NESEP) 2

Nike company 16

Noriko Takahashi **35**

Nummela, A. 68

O

overspeed training 67-69

overstriding 28-29

P

Paavolainen, L. 68

pace, average training 72

Padilla, Doug 72, 130

pelvis position 30

performance blueprint 101-102*f*

performances/racing
attitude towards 104, 106
environmental demands assessment 133, 135*f*
event demands assessment 129-130, 135*f*
factors influencing 101-102*f*
functional demands assessment 130, 135*f*
goals 113-114, 125-129, 126*t*, 128*t*
logistical demands assessment 132, 135*f*
mental demands assessment 132, 135*f*
peak 87-90
physical demands assessment 130-131, 135*f*
postevent evaluation 114-115, 140, 143*f*, 144*f*, 145*f*, 146*f*
predicting results 126*t*-129, 128*t*
preparation example 117-122
preparation for 123-146, 149
prerace planning 133-142*f*, 134*f*, 135*f*, 136*f*, 137*f*, 139*f*, 141*f*
self-concept and 106-108
situational assessment 103-104
social demands assessment 132, 135*f*
technical demands assessment 133, 135*f*

personal identity 92-97, 109-112

Petruna, Ellie 3

physical activation 104

physical demands assessment 130-131, 135*f*

plyometric energy 38-39, 68-69

Poole, Craig 32

postevent evaluation 114-115, 140, 143*f*, 144*f*, 145*f*, 146*f*

posture 31-32, **34**-37, **35, 36**

power, running 67-69

predicting race times 126-129, 126*t*, 128*t*

preparation, race
examples 8, 117-122
goal-setting 125-129, 126*t*, 128*t*
steps in 123-124

prerace planning 133-142*f*,
    134*f*, 135*f*, 136*f*, 137*f*, 139*f*,
    141*f*
pronation 33
psychomechanics
    audiogenics 54-55, 56, 62,
        89-90
    committment to improving
        47-48
    effects of 70-71
    Miller's first experience with
        10
    non-traditional methods 55-60
    training using 76-77
    visualization 51-52, 54-55, 76

R

race preparation
    examples 8, 117-122
    goal-setting 125-129, 126*t*,
        128*t*
    steps in 123-124
races, road 7
racing. *See* performances/racing
recovery phase (stride) 25, **26,
    27**
repetition 76
"rhino breathing" 41
Rono, Henry 24-25
"Running Economy,
    Anthropometric
    Dimensions, and
    Kinematic Variables" 32
running poems 56
running technique 25-28, **26, 27**
Rusko, H.U. 68
Ryun, Jim **26-27**

S

Schechter, B. 66
Schiesser, Edie 148
Scooter, Stride-Rite 59-**60**, 75
"The Secrets of Speed" 41
self-concept and performance
    106-108, 109-112

Self Esteem 92
self-esteem 92-97
self-talk, positive 54-55, 81-83,
    89
Sheehan, George 31
Shorter, Frank 5, **6**, 38
shoulders 32
sightseeing runs 73, **74**
situational self-esteem 95
sleep factors 72-73, 130
Smith, Ina 148
social demands assessment
    132, 135*f*
Sonne, Liz 12-14
speed
    and distance 71-73
    improving 61-64, 66-67
sport psychology 11
Staton, Laurie 89
strength, leg 67-69
stress response, psycho-
    physiological 103-104
stride length/frequency 28-30,
    66-67
stride mechanics
    arm action **26, 27**, 32, 33, 39-
        40, 55-57, 67
    efficiency 23-24, 33, 45
    foot plant **26**, 33, 59-**60**
    posture 31-32, **34**-37, **35, 36**
    sequence 78
stride phases 25-28, **26, 27**
Stride-Rite Scooter 59-**60**, 75
success stories 147-148
supplementary energy sources
    38-40
support phase (stride) **26, 27,**
    28
Swing-Rite Harness 55-**58**
Syracuse University 1

T

technical demands assessment
    133, 135*f*
tempo runs 73

timing
  evaluating performance by
    111, 113
  track intervals 86-87
toeing off 39, 77
track training 61-64, 86-87
training. *See also* preparation
  comprehensiveness of 114
  cross-training (cycling) 70-
    71, 75
  endurance training 71-73
  methods 73-76
  overspeed training 67-69
  pacing during 72
  and psychomechanics 76-77
  track training 61-64, 86-87
  videotaping during 48-50, 120
turnover rates, stride. *See* stride
  length/frequency

U

University of Utah 11-14

V

values, personal 109
Vega, Teodoro **34**
videotaping, use of 48-50, 120
Vietnam 4-5
visualization 51-52, 54-55

W

Wagner, Debbie 148
Wahlquist, Linda "Hooper" 148
Walker, Jim 67
Webb, Alan **107**
Wilmore, Jack 39
World Blind Marathon
    Championship 14, 16-20

Y

Yessis, Michael 66

Z

Zachariassen, __ 90

About the Author

Thomas S. Miller is a recognized expert in performance enhancement for endurance sports, both in mechanics and motivation. A veteran of more than 100 marathons, he holds a doctorate in exercise and sport science with an emphasis in performance psychology. He writes articles for several top publications, including *Runner's World*.

Miller has coached such notable athletes as five-time world triathlon champion Joann Garrucio; masters world cycling stage race champion Dirk Cowley; world blind marathon champion Harry Cordellos; the U.S. Disabled Cross Country Ski Team; and John Cahill, who at age 73 ran a marathon in 3:05. A self-described "blue-collar coach," Miller says he most enjoys coaching "real people" who have full-time jobs, families, and responsibilities.

A former member of the United States Marine Corps, Miller received silver and bronze stars for his combat heroism and leadership as a platoon leader in Vietnam. He now owns RiTeKnologies and teaches at the University of Phoenix. Miller resides in Salt Lake City, Utah, where he enjoys running, cycling, rowing, and Nordic skiing.

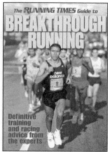